S0-ADS-812

13-Digit ISBN: 978-1-60433-209-4
10-Digit ISBN: 1-60433-209-3

This book may be ordered by mail from the publisher. Please include $2.50 for postage and handling.
Please support your local bookseller first!

Books published by Cider Mill Press Book Publishers are available at special discounts for bulk purchases in the United States by corporations, institutions, and other organizations. For more information, please contact the publisher.

Cider Mill Press Book Publishers
"Where good books are ready for press"
12 Port Farm Road
Kennebunkport, Maine 04046

Visit us on the Web!
www.cidermillpress.com

Design by Tilly Grassa, TGCreative Services
Typography: Century Gothic, Allstar, Marcelle Script

1 2 3 4 5 6 7 8 9 0

Dedicated to Mom, Dad,
Paul, Michael, Heather
and all of the baseball fans in
Canton, Massachusetts.

Contents

Foreword

In 2008, Ripken Baseball purchased a Single-A team in the Florida State League and moved the franchise to Port Charlotte. We were excited to add another club into our ownership group, which also included the Aberdeen IronBirds and Augusta GreenJackets. After assembling a front office staff in Port Charlotte, we came to the obvious question—what do we name our new team?

We felt the team name was one of the most important decisions we had to make. How unique should the name be? Can we connect it to an aspect of the community? What will the logo look like?

Our discussions about the team name were energetic and passionate. I pushed strongly to have the word "crabs" included in our new brand. I grew up in Maryland, an area famous for crabs. Plus, I thought it was catchy and our fans would love it. We did a lot of research and named the team the Charlotte Stone Crabs.

Stone Crabs worked well because this type of crab is indigenous to the Port Charlotte region. Also, Devil Rays (the original name of our Major League affiliate, the Tampa Bay Rays) eat stone crabs. So, the Stone Crabs are a "feeder" for the Rays in more than one way!

There's the story behind the Charlotte Stone Crabs moniker. This book, *Root for the Home Team: Minor League Baseball's Most Off-the-Wall Team Names and the Stories Behind Them,* tells you the origins behind many other unique team names throughout the history of Minor League Baseball.

Bill Ripken
Co-Chairman & Executive VP
Ripken Baseball, Inc.

Introduction

One of the joys of being a broadcaster in the minor leagues is talking baseball with people scattered throughout the country. Whether the conversation is with a casual observer or an obsessed fan, the question I'm asked the most is "what is with those wacky team names in the minors?"

The quirky names across uniforms have been a part of Minor League Baseball for over a century. Team names can honor an aspect of a community, create enthusiasm for the local fans and give their squad a unique brand.

Many older team names originated from the sportswriter covering the team, like the Sioux Falls Canaries. They got their moniker when the local scribe wrote about their yellow uniforms resembling canaries' feathers. In the 1970s–1980s, many teams shifted and took the name of their Major League affiliate, reminding fans of clubs like the Bakersfield Dodgers and Pawtucket Red Sox that their players could soon be Major League stars.

The unique-team-name boom struck the minor leagues in the early 1990s when executives noticed new-logoed merchandise sales skyrocketed. The Montgomery Biscuits shipped at least one team cap order to all 50 states in the year after introducing the team logo.

Now, almost every minor league team has its own individual brand. Players drafted by the Los Angeles Angels of Anaheim likely go on to play for the Orem Owlz, Cedar Rapids Kernels, Inland Empire 66ers, Arkansas Travelers and Salt Lake Bees on their path to the majors.

From the Everett AquaSox to the Yazoo City Zoos, I hope you enjoy this book.

Tim Hagerty

MOBILE OYSTER GRABBERS

League: Southern Interstate League
City: Mobile, AL
Years: 1903

Mobile Oyster Grabbers Turn Back the Clock Day
—Courtesy of Mobile BayBears

Mobile, Alabama's first professional team had the city's most unique baseball nickname to date. For just one season, Mobile's team in the Southern Interstate League was called the Oyster Grabbers. An oyster grabber is a tong-like device fishermen use to reach into shallow water and gather oysters. Set right on Mobile Bay, this city has often used gulf-styled nicknames for its professional baseball teams, like the Mobile Sea Gulls, Mobile Oystermen, Mobile BaySharks and Mobile BayBears. The Oyster Grabbers were honored in 2007 on turn back the clock day in Mobile, when the Double-A BayBears donned the jerseys of Mobile's original team.

Not to Be Confused With: Providence Clamdiggers, Hickory Crawdads, Newport Pearl Diggers, Morgan City Oyster Shuckers

Between the Lines: Mobile and Atlanta agreed to swing at every good pitch as an experiment on September 19, 1910. The game lasted only 32 minutes and Mobile won, 2-1.

MONTGOMERY BISCUITS

League: Southern League
City: Montgomery, AL
Years: 2004-Present

When the team nickname now considered by many the most quirky of all unique minor league team names was announced, it was greeted with silence. In May of 2003, at Montgomery's Jubilee City Fest, a local disc jockey named "Big Bubba" announced Montgomery's new Southern League team would be called the Biscuits. After this announcement, Big Bubba and all other dignitaries on stage stared at a silent, disappointed crowd. Since then, the Biscuits team name has grown on fans in Alabama's capital city. The official Biscuits team slogan is "History in the Baking," and the Biscuits media guide describes the official team colors as "Butter and Blue."

Not to Be Confused With: Eau Claire Puffs

Between the Lines: Led by current Major League stars Evan Longoria, Reid Brignac and Evan Meek, the Biscuits won Southern League championships in 2006 and 2007.

 Arizona

 Arkansas

TUCSON LIZARDS

League: Arizona-Texas League
City: Tucson, AZ
Years: 1932

The Tucson Lizards slithered through the Class D Arizona-Texas League against the Bisbee Bees and Phoenix Senators. Dozens of different lizards call the Arizona desert home. Instead of a more specific name like the Canyon Spotted Whiptails or Elegant Earless Lizards, team management stuck with Lizards for the team name, to include all types of lizard species in the Sonoran Desert area.

Not to Be Confused With:
Yuma Bullfrogs, Kissimmee Cobras

Between the Lines: According to Tucson baseball legend, a Lizards outfielder once sprinted back to the dugout in fear because he spotted a live rattlesnake in the outfield at Randolph Baseball Park in Tucson.

FAYETTEVILLE EDUCATORS

League: Arkansas State League
City: Fayetteville, AR
Years: 1934

The boys of summer went to summer school with this team name. The Fayetteville Educators decided upon their academic title to honor the University of Arkansas, located in Fayetteville. The Educators received failing grades in their first season, finishing in last place in the Class D Arkansas State League against the Bentonville Officeholders, Siloam Springs Buffaloes and Rogers Rustlers.

Not to Be Confused With: Sherman-Denison Students

Between the Lines: Fayetteville's George Bender holds the Arkansas State League record for complete games with 24.

NORTHWEST ARKANSAS NATURALS

League: Texas League
City: Springdale, AR
Years: 2008- Present

The newest team in the Double-A Texas League took its name after the state nickname for Arkansas. The "Natural State" now houses the Northwest Arkansas Naturals. The nickname was a natural fit for the area, and fans agreed, selecting Naturals over other candidates in a name the team contest that included Thunder Chickens, Anglers, Monarchs, Ridgerunners, Highlanders and Bass.

Not to Be Confused With: Washington Wild Things

Between the Lines: Slugger Clint Robinson won the Texas League Triple Crown in 2010 for the Naturals and led the team to a Double-A championship.

PINE BLUFF JUDGES

League: Cotton States League
City: Pine Bluff, AR
Years: 1930-1940, 1950-1955

1930 Pine Bluff Judges
—National Baseball Hall of Fame Library. Cooperstown, NY

The Pine Bluff Judges probably had a great relationship with umpires in the Class D Cotton States League. After 22 years without professional baseball, the Judges selected a legal themed name because fans expressed positive reviews of a former team name in the Class D Arkansas-Texas League, the Pine Bluff Barristers. The Barristers also took their name from the courtroom; a barrister is a type of lawyer.

Not to Be Confused With: Frankfort Lawmakers

Between the Lines: Hugh Lott and Vachel Perkins combined to throw an early season no-hitter for the Judges against the Hot Springs Bathers on April 20, 1951.

California

BAKERSFIELD BLAZE

League: California League
City: Bakersfield, CA
Years: 1995-Present

The Bakersfield Blaze team name originates from a legendary story in California League lore. In 1982, the Bakersfield Mariners played Visalia late into the night. As midnight approached, the sprinkler timers struck and the field was flooded with water. The grounds crew finally shut the sprinklers off but the grass was covered in puddles. Visalia manager Phil Roof suggested igniting the field with fire to dry the puddles. The plan worked, the game resumed, and 13 years after the field was set ablaze a new team name was born.

Not to Be Confused With: Phoenix Firebirds

Between the Lines: The Blaze start summertime games at 7:30 or 7:45 because of sun delays. Sam Lynn Ballpark is built facing the sunset, causing the sunlight to directly face home plate at 7:05, and batters would not be able to see at that time.

FRESNO RAISIN EATERS

League: Pacific Coast League
City: Fresno, CA
Years: 1906

Raisin lovers around the globe have Fresno, California, to thank. Fresno and the surrounding towns in central California produce 60 percent of the raisins in the world. The connection between raisins and California's fifth-largest city brings us one of the most unique team names in Pacific Coast League history, the Fresno Raisin Eaters. Fresno only played under the name Raisin Eaters for one season, but over a century later to the quirky moniker was introduced to a new generation of baseball fans, when the Triple-A Fresno Grizzlies wore the jerseys of the Raisin Eaters each Wednesday during the 2006 season.

Not to Be Confused With:
Kalamazoo Celery Eaters,
Bay City Rice Eaters, Merced Fig Growers

Between the Lines: September 2, 1906 is a day Raisin Eaters fans would like to forget. Oakland Oaks pitcher Eli Cates threw a no-hitter against Fresno that day.

**Fresno Raisin Eaters
Turn Back the Clock Day**
—Courtesy of
Fresno Grizzlies

MODESTO NUTS

League: California League
City: Modesto, CA
Years: 2005-Present

Modesto changed Major League affiliates after the 2004 season from Oakland to Colorado, so the Modesto A's team name no longer fit. The front office polled the public on prospective team names, with Nuts, Dusters, Steel, Derailers and Strike as choices. Nuts garnered 52 percent of the support and the Modesto Nuts were born. Modesto is known for almond and walnut production, and the area is home to Blue Diamond, a widely recognized nut supplier.

Not to Be Confused With: Allentown Peanuts, New London Planters

Between the Lines: Ubaldo Jimenez and Troy Tulowitzki were Major League All-Stars together for the Colorado Rockies in 2010. Five years earlier, they helped the Modesto Nuts reach the playoffs.

MUDVILLE NINE

League: California League
City: Stockton, CA
Years: 2000-2001

Poetry met reality in 2000 when the Mudville Nine first took the field in the Single-A California League. The Mudville Nine were named after the fictitious team profiled in Ernest Thayer's poem "Casey at the Bat." At the time, Thayer said his ode was not based on an actual team, but some have speculated "Casey at the Bat" was written about the Stockton team in the California League in 1888, which Thayer covered as a sports writer.

Not to Be Confused With:
Danville 97s

Between the Lines:
The 2001 Mudville Nine had a great season, advancing to the playoffs, where they lost to the Bakersfield Blaze in the first round.

OAKLAND DUDES

League: California League
City: Oakland, CA
Years: 1899-1900

When the Oakland Dudes took the field the word *dude* had a different meaning than it does now. Today you may use it as an informal greeting, but in the 1800s when Americans were moving west, the word dude specifically referred to someone on a ranch in the west. The Oakland Dudes played other uniquely named California League teams at their home ranch, like the San Francisco Friscos and San Jose Prune Pickers.

Not to Be Confused With: Long Beach Beachcombers

Between the Lines: If you thought the baseball season was long these days, consider the Oakland Dudes 1899 season—they played for nine months! The California League schedule went from March to November back then.

PETALUMA INCUBATORS

League: Central California League
City: Petaluma, CA
Years: 1910

The Petaluma Incubators tried to enclose the rest of the Class D Central California League in 1910, playing against opponents like the Healdsburg Grapevines and Santa Rosa Prune Pickers. The Incubators nickname was a prideful one for the area, as the Petaluma Incubator Factory was the largest one in the world around the turn of the 20th century.

Not to Be Confused With: Leaksville-Draper-Spray Triplets

Between the Lines: A few miles from where the Incubators once played, Oakland A's outfielder Jonny Gomes practiced hitting in a barn converted to a batting cage.

RANCHO CUCAMONGA QUAKES

League: California League
City: Rancho Cucamonga, CA
Years: 1993-Present

Some teams may shy away from admitting their ballpark is near an earthquake causing thrust fault, but the Rancho Cucamonga Quakes embrace their location. Rancho Cucamonga, California, is set along the Cucamonga-Sierra Madre fault, and the local professional baseball team is sprinkled with earthquake references. The Quakes play their games at the Epicenter, and the team mascots are named Tremor and Aftershock.

Not to Be Confused With: Salem Avalanche, Trenton Thunder, Salem-Keizer Volcanoes

Between the Lines: Over 500 people camped out on the street the morning tickets went on sale to the Quakes first home game on March 15, 1993.

SALINAS PEPPERS

League: Western League
City: Salinas, CA
Years: 1995-1997

The Salinas Peppers played in the Salinas Valley of California, a heavily agricultural area known for wine vineyards and pepper farms. The Peppers had the best record in the Western League in 1995, their inaugural year playing an independent circuit that also featured the Bend Bandits and Sonoma County Crushers.

Not to Be Confused With: Davenport Onion Weeders, Griffin Pimientos

Between the Lines: Ben Weber became the greatest success story from the Peppers roster, going on to pitch six seasons in the Major Leagues, including four outings in the 2002 World Series for the champion Anaheim Angels.

VISALIA RAWHIDE

League: California League
City: Visalia, CA
Years: 2009-Present

With both baseballs and baseball gloves containing leather, the name Rawhide would fit any professional baseball team. For the Single-A Visalia Rawhide, the brand fits even closer because of the agriculture and dairy community in Visalia. Recreation Park hosts an annual Dairy Day Game that features between-inning farm-themed events including a players-only cow milking contest. The team's identity before the Visalia Rawhide was the Visalia Oaks, who took their name from the sequoia trees in the area.

Not to Be Confused With: Shelby Farmers

Between the Lines: Rawhide fans enjoyed an early Halloween in May 2011, when the club held a "Candy Drop" promotion, dumping 700 pounds of candy from a helicopter after a game against the High Desert Mavericks.

COLORADO SPRINGS MILLIONAIRES

League: Western League
City: Colorado Springs, CO
Years: 1901-1905, 1912, 1916

1904 Colorado Springs Millionaires
—National Baseball Hall of Fame Library. Cooperstown, NY

The Colorado Springs Millionaires played long before the era of seven-digit player salaries. The team took its name from gold rushes that drove people to Colorado Springs to try to strike it big. The Pikes Peak Gold Rush brought over 100,000 people to the territory now known as Colorado in the 1850s. Thirty years later W.S. Stratton and others took advantage of the Cripple Creek Gold Discovery, and suddenly new millionaires, and a team named Millionaires, were springing up in Colorado Springs. These days, the Triple-A Colorado Springs Sky Sox play at Security Service Field, the stadium with the highest elevation in American professional baseball.

Not to Be Confused With: Spartanburg Traders

Between the Lines: The fleet-of-foot Rabbit Nill scored the most runs in the Western League (117) for the Millionaires in 1904. Nill went on to play five seasons in the Major Leagues with the Washington Senators and Cleveland Naps.

Connecticut

Delaware

WATERBURY AUTHORS

League: Connecticut League
City: Waterbury, CT
Years: 1906-1908

1908 Waterbury Authors
—National Baseball Hall of Fame Library,
Cooperstown, NY

The Waterbury Authors of the Class B Connecticut League honored the area's literary history. Authors Mark Twain, Harriet Beecher Stowe and Noah Webster (of dictionary fame) all lived in Connecticut. If the nickname Authors doesn't strike you as fierce, consider that Waterbury played against the Bridgeport Orators. Waterbury is titled the "Brass City," and is noted for producing watches and clocks. This influenced Waterbury's team in the 1947 Class B Colonial League, the Waterbury Timers.

Not to Be Confused With: New Haven Profs

Between the Lines: Authors pitcher Ed Farley wrote his name into the history book on July 19, 1907, throwing a no-hitter against Bridgeport.

WILMINGTON QUICKSTEPS

League: Interstate Association
City: Wilmington, DE
Years: 1883-1884

You see more on-field dancing in football than you do in baseball, but there was a Minor League Baseball team in the late 1800s named after a dance step. The Wilmington Quicksteps tried to skip past the Reading Actives, Brooklyn Grays and the rest of the Interstate Association in 1883. Off the field and on the dance floor, the Quickstep is a fast-paced ballroom dance, similar to a Foxtrot. These days, the Wilmington Blue Rocks play in the Single-A Carolina League, taking their name after the blue granite found along the Brandywine Creek in Wilmington.

Not to Be Confused With: Griffin Lightfoots

Between the Lines: Joe Simmons brought great wisdom to the helm of the Quicksteps, having played three seasons in the Major Leagues, but Simmons was on the hot seat in 1884, winning just two of the 18 games he managed.

Florida

LAKELAND FLYING TIGERS

League: Florida State League
City: Lakeland, FL
Years: 2007-Present

Joker Marchant Stadium—home of the Flying Tigers. —Courtesy of Brian Merzbach

The addition of an adjective to this team name vaulted it from ordinary to unique. From the beginning of their affiliation with the Detroit Tigers in 1967, Lakeland's team was known as the Lakeland Tigers. To add some flavor, and to pay homage to a local aeronautics school, the team was renamed the Lakeland Flying Tigers before the 2007 season. Lakeland, Florida, was once home to the Lakeland School of Aeronautics, where over 8,000 pilots were trained in the 1940s. The school was located on the site now occupied by Joker Marchant Stadium, home of the Flying Tigers.

Not to Be Confused With: Rhode Island Tiger Sharks, Lancaster JetHawks

Between the Lines: The Flying Tigers grabbed national headlines on September 1, 2010, when they didn't allow a hit until the 14th inning! Cole Nelson, Bruce Rondon and Matt Little all threw hitless outings in Lakeland's eventual 17-inning victory.

MIAMI AMIGOS

League: Inter-American League
City: Miami, FL
Years: 1979

There was no concern about team chemistry in the Miami Amigos clubhouse. The Amigos played in the Triple-A Inter-American League, a league created to provide an international base to Minor League Baseball. The Amigos team name symbolized a connection between American and International baseball, with Miami befriending teams like the Caracas Metropolitanos and Puerto Rico Boricuas.

Not to Be Confused With: Palestine Pals

Between the Lines: The most promising prospect the Amigos produced was their manager, Davey Johnson. Seven years after leading the Amigos to a first place finish, he managed the 1986 New York Mets to a World Series title.

MIAMI WAHOOS

League: Florida East Coast League
City: Miami, FL
Years: 1940-1941

Hall of Famer Max Carey managed the Miami Wahoos in 1940
—Library of Congress photo

Miami's Major League Baseball team is named after a fish, but the Miami Marlins aren't the first aquatic named professional baseball team to call Miami home. The Miami Wahoos were named after the dark blue fish found in tropical regions like south Florida. While it sounds like a goofy name for a professional baseball team, the wahoo is actually an intimidating fish, growing up to eight feet in length with the ability to swim 60 miles per hour.

Not to Be Confused With: Taunton Herrings, Madison Muskies, Victoria Mussels

Between the Lines: The best pitcher on the 1940 Wahoos was also one of their youngest. Bobby Hogue was 19-years-old when he pitched for the Wahoos, and advanced to the Major Leagues where he pitched for the Boston Braves, New York Yankees and St. Louis Browns.

ATLANTA CRACKERS

League: Southern League
City: Atlanta, GA
Years: 1895-1896, 1903-1965

Baseball fans in Atlanta hoped the Crackers didn't crumble down the stretch. The Atlanta Crackers team name actually had nothing to do with edible snacks. The Crackers team name was shortened from Firecrackers, the label Atlanta's team in 1892 used. Other Minor League Baseball teams in Atlanta's history have included the Atlanta Atlantas and Atlanta Firemen.

1938 Atlanta Crackers
—National Baseball Hall of Fame Library, Cooperstown, NY

Not to Be Confused With: Crisfield Crabbers

Between the Lines: The Atlanta Crackers completed the first, and only, player for broadcaster trade. The Crackers wanted Brooklyn Dodgers minor league catcher Cliff Dapper, and the Dodgers wanted Crackers broadcaster Ernie Harwell, so the two teams swapped Dapper for Harwell in 1948.

COLUMBUS BABIES

League: Southern League
City: Columbus, GA
Years: 1896

The Columbus Babies didn't get their team name from whining at umpires calls. The Babies were the newest team in the Southern League in 1896, and were called the Babies because of their inexperience compared to seasoned teams like the Birmingham Bluebirds. Other Columbus team names have included the Columbus RedStixx and Columbus Confederate Yankees.

Not to Be Confused With: Fall River Adopted Sons

Between the Lines: The Babies roster featured eight future big leaguers, including pitcher Roscoe Miller, who led the American League in assists by a pitcher (112) for the 1901 Detroit Tigers.

Mike Kahoe played for the Columbus Babies in 1896 —Library of Congress photo

MACON PEACHES

League: South Atlantic League
City: Macon, GA
Years: 1908-1915, 1923-1930, 1932, 1936-1942, 1946-1955, 1961-1964, 1966-1967, 1980-1982

Luther Williams Field—former home of the Macon Peaches
—Courtesy of Brian Merzbach

The professional baseball team in Georgia's sixth-largest city has been called the Peaches on and off for a century. Georgia produces hundreds of millions of pounds worth of peaches per year. The most recent professional baseball team in Macon was the Macon Music, paying tribute to musician natives like Otis Redding, The Allman Brothers and Little Richard, as well as a reference to the Macon-based Georgia Music Hall of Fame.

Not to Be Confused With: Wilmington Peach Growers, Mission Grapefruiters, San Leandro Cherry Pickers

Between the Lines: The Peaches threw a no-hitter in 1930 with seven pitchers. Each threw one hitless frame in the seven-inning contest. There has never been a seven pitcher no-hitter in the Major Leagues.

SAVANNAH SAND GNATS

League: South Atlantic League
City: Savannah, GA
Years: 1996-Present

Management of the Savannah Cardinals didn't expect to change their team name in 1996, but a last-minute shift in affiliations to the Dodgers had them scrambling to change their identity. Instead of using the Dodgers name, the club wanted a lively new name connecting the team to Savannah. A panel of fans was created to narrow down name suggestions, and Savannah Sand Gnats was the winner. Sand gnats are insects most often found flying above salt water marshes on the Georgia coast.

Not to Be Confused With:
Gary Sand Fleas, Milford Sandpipers

Between the Lines: The Sand Gnats hired Ted Batchelor in 2010 to run the bases between innings—while on fire. Batchelor is the Guinness human world record holder for being on fire the longest (two hours and 57 minutes, for those of you keeping score at home).

SOUTH GEORGIA PEANUTS

League: South Coast League
City: Albany, GA
Years: 2007

While nearby Dothan, Alabama, is proclaimed the "Peanut Capital of the World," it is Albany, Georgia, that claimed the South Georgia Peanuts of the South Coast League. Their debut season featured opponents like the Aiken Foxhounds and Bradenton Juice. The Peanuts sold a variety of peanuts at the concession stands during their inaugural season.

Not to Be Confused With:
Idaho Falls Nuggets,
Santa Ana Walnut Growers

Between the Lines: The Peanuts made national news in 2007 for not playing. After a bench-clearing brawl with the Macon Music, the Peanuts walked off the field, refusing to play and accepting a forfeit.

Wally Backman managed the South Georgia Peanuts in 2007
—Tom Ryder, Binghamton Mets photo

WAYCROSS BLOWHARDS

League: Empire State League
City: Waycross, GA
Years: 1913

The Waycross Blowhards boasted their way through the Class D Empire State League against the Cordele Babies and Americus Muckalees, a team named after nearby Muckalee Creek. In 1906 the Waycross Machinists beat the Columbus River Snipes and the Valdosta Stars and finished first in the Class D Georgia State League. There was no professional baseball in Waycross until the Blowhards in 1913, and the team name was believed to be a result of the city bragging about its 1906 championship.

Not to Be Confused With: Coffeyville Glassblowers

Between the Lines: Being no-hit is bad enough, but the Blowhards were held hitless twice in one day! Dana Fillingim threw a no-hitter in game one of a doubleheader on July 23, 1913, and his Cordele teammate Percy Wilder accomplished the same feat in game two.

WAIKIKI BEACH BOYS

League: Hawaii Winter Baseball
City: Honolulu, HI
Years: 2006-2008

The Waikiki Beach Boys team name rode the wave of support for Hawaii's most well known surfing family. Duane Kahanamoku and his friends started their own surfing club at Waikiki Beach in 1905 called Hui Nalu. Kahanamoku and his friends are now known in Hawaiian history as the "Waikiki Beach Boys," and are given credit for revitalizing surfing in Hawaii. From 2006-2008 the Waikiki Beach Boys carved against the North Shore Honu, West Oahu CaneFires and Honolulu Sharks.

Not to Be Confused With: Traverse City Beach Bums, Corpus Christi Beach Dawgs

Between the Lines: Nate Schierholtz played for the Beach Boys in 2006 and later went 1-for-5 with an RBI in the 2010 World Series for the San Francisco Giants.

Idaho

IDAHO FALLS SPUDS

League: Utah-Idaho League
City: Idaho Falls, ID
Years: 1926-1928

1927 Idaho Falls Spuds
—National Baseball Hall of Fame Library. Cooperstown, NY

Quick, think of the one state you'd expect to have a team named after potatoes. The Idaho Falls Spuds played just miles north of Blackfoot, Idaho, still known as "The Potato Capital of the World." Cities outside Idaho were also proud of their potato production, with Parksley, Virginia, and La Grange, Georgia, also having professional baseball teams named "Spuds" at one time. Idaho Falls still uses a team name indigenous to the Gem State, going by the Idaho Falls Chukars. A chukar is a pheasant like bird, known for its speed.

Not to Be Confused With: Carlsbad Potashers, Corsicana Gumbo Busters

Between the Lines: Idaho Falls had a game suspended in Butte, Montana, because of snowfall on August 22, 1992. It was the first summer snow-out in the history of the Pioneer League.

POCATELLO GEMS

League: Pioneer League
City: Pocatello, ID
Years: 1984-1985

Halliwell Field—former home of the Pocatello Gems
—Courtesy of Brian Merzbach

References to the diamond had a double meaning for fans of the Pocatello Gems. The rookie-level squad took their name after Idaho, known as the Gem State.

Decades before the Helena Gold Sox beat the Gems and the rest of the Pioneer League for the 1984 championship, the Pocatello Bannocks joined the 1926 Class C Utah-Idaho League. After stints of taking the names of their Major League affiliates, Pocatello's professional baseball team got a nickname upgrade, with the Pocatello Posse taking the field in "America's Smile Capital" for the 1993 Pioneer League season.

Not to Be Confused With: Eugene Emeralds

Between the Lines: The greatest player to wear a Gems uniform was Walt Weiss, who hit .310 for Pocatello in 1985 and three seasons later was playing in the World Series for the Oakland Athletics.

Illinois

AURORA HOODOOS

League: Illinois-Indiana League
City: Aurora, IL
Years: 1892

Ernest Thayer was probably a member of the Aurora Hoodoos fan club. Four years after baseball's most famous poem "Casey at the Bat" was written by Thayer, Aurora's team in the Illinois-Indiana League borrowed a piece of the composition for their team name. In some versions of the poem two players are referred to when it reads "the former was a hoodoo and the latter was a cake."

Not to Be Confused With: Waterloo Lulus

Between the Lines: When the Peoria Canaries relocated and became the Aurora Hoodoos in 1892, Mike Trost was their manager. He played in the Major Leagues before managing the Hoodoos in 1890 and again after his stint as a manager in 1895.

CENTRALIA ZEROS

League: Mississippi-Ohio Valley League
City: Centralia, IL
Years: 1951-1952

Centralia Zeros pitcher Lee Tunnison led the Class D Mississippi-Ohio Valley League in strikeouts in 1951, but this team name had nothing to do with the zeros Tunnison was putting up on the scoreboard. Centralia is set where the two original branches of the Illinois Central Railroad meet, so its measurement on the railroad location is zero.

Not to Be Confused With: Oklahoma City 89ers

Between the Lines: Centralia player Lou Bekeza won a pregame cow milking contest against his Paducah Chiefs rival Walter DeFreitas in 1950. The cow kicked DeFreitas, rendering him unavailable to play.

FREEPORT PRETZELS

League: Wisconsin State League
City: Freeport, IL
Years: 1905-1910, 1911

Freeport, Illinois, has been known as "Pretzel City, USA," since the Billerbeck Bakery spread pretzels throughout the region in 1869. Decades after this distribution, the Freeport Pretzels first played in the Class D Wisconsin State League in 1905. The Pretzels were the only team outside the state of Wisconsin in this circuit, trying to salt opponents like the Beloit Collegians and Wausau Lumberjacks. By 1910 the Pretzels had moved to the Class D Northern Association, where opponents included the Muscatine Pearl Finders, Sterling Infants and Clinton Teddies.

1909 Freeport Pretzels
—National Baseball Hall of Fame Library.
Cooperstown, NY

Not to Be Confused With: Lebanon Pretzel Eaters

Between the Lines: Over 5,000 fans came to watch the pennant deciding game between the Pretzels and the La Crosse Pinks on September 1, 1906. The Pinks broke a scoreless tie in the 10th inning and won the game.

JOLIET SLAMMERS

League: Frontier League
City: Joliet, IL
Years: 2011-Present

In 2011, the Joliet Slammers broke out one of the best team names in years and also locked in the Best New Logo Award from Ballpark Digest. The Joliet Correctional Center closed in 2002 but it remains a tourist attraction. The parking lot in front of the prison is a tourism shop that grabs a lot of business from people traveling along Route 66. The Joliet Correctional Center is just one mile from Silver Cross Field, the home of the Slammers. In addition to its use as a prison phrase, Slammers has a baseball connection, referring to a grand slam.

Not to Be Confused With: Pawtucket Slaters

Between the Lines: The Slammers beat the River City Rascals three games to one to capture the 2011 Frontier League Championship Series.

LINCOLN ABES

League: Illinois-Missouri League
City: Lincoln, IL
Years: 1910-1914

While the state capital is named after the 16th President, Nebraska has never had a baseball team named after Abraham Lincoln. The Lincoln Abes actually played in Illinois, in the Class D Illinois-Missouri League. Campaigning against the Champaign

1911 Lincoln Abes
—National Baseball Hall of Fame Library.
Cooperstown, NY

Velvets and Streator Speedboys, the Abes finished first in 1912. During this time, the Lincoln Railsplitters played in Nebraska's capital city, trying to run down the St. Joseph Drummers and Topeka Kaws in the Western League.

Not to Be Confused With: Springfield Governors, Harrisburg Senators

Between the Lines: The Abes' best hitter was Polly Wolfe. He had 164 hits to lead the team, earning himself a cup of coffee in the Major Leagues, playing nine games for the Chicago White Sox from 1912-1914.

EVANSVILLE TRIPLETS

League: American Association
City: Evansville, IN
Years: 1970-1984

Bosse Field—former home of the Evansville Triplets
—Courtesy of Evansville Otters

Evansville is situated where Illinois, Indiana and Kentucky meet, and is considered the center of this tri-state area. The Evansville Triplets were named after the city's geographic positioning, and first used the name Triplets in the Triple-A American Association. Evansville is set on the banks of the Ohio River and is known as the "River City." This city nickname made the Evansville River Rats team nickname also seem appropriate, when they swam through the Three-I League in 1901.

Not to Be Confused With: Tri-City ValleyCats

Between the Lines: Fans saw some remarkable players in the 15-year history of the Triplets. Hall of Fame pitcher Bert Blyleven once struck out 17 in a game for Evansville, and Jim Leyland managed the Triplets to the championship in 1979.

FORT WAYNE TINCAPS

League: Midwest League
City: Fort Wayne, IN
Years: 2009-Present

The Fort Wayne TinCaps name comes from Johnny Appleseed, who was known for wearing a cooking pot on his head during his travels throughout the Midwest. Appleseed is buried in Fort Wayne, where they still celebrate his contributions with the Johnny Appleseed Festival each September.

Not to Be Confused With: DeLand Sun Caps

Between the Lines: The 2009 TinCaps won 94 games, the most in all of Minor League Baseball. Only the Los Angeles Angels of Anaheim, Los Angeles Dodgers and New York Yankees had more wins in all of organized baseball that season.

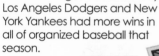

F O R T   W A Y N E

MUNCIE FRUIT JARS

League: Interstate Association
City: Muncie, IN
Years: 1906, 1908

Before you go into disbelief about Muncie, Indiana's baseball team being called the Fruit Jars in the early 1900s, consider that until 2002, you could visit the Phillip Robinson Fruit Jar Museum in downtown Muncie. The Fruit Jars left the field after just one season in the Interstate Association, falling behind the Flint Vehics. They were put back on the shelf in 1908 in the Class C Indiana-Ohio League, finishing behind the Richmond Quakers. As for the World's Largest (and only?) Fruit Jar Museum, it closed in 2002 after failing to secure the proper insurance.

Not to Be Confused With: Boise Fruit Pickers, Okmulgee Glassblowers

Between the Lines: Fruit Jars manager Fred Paige had the most normal name among skippers in the league. Bootie Wolf managed the team from Saginaw and Peaches O'Neill managed in Anderson.

SOUTH BEND SILVER HAWKS

League: Midwest League
City: South Bend, IN
Years: 1994-Present

Their mascot is a growling bird with a baseball cap, but the South Bend Silver Hawks are actually named after a car. The Studebaker Silver Hawk was produced from 1957 to 1959 at the Studebaker headquarters in South Bend. Forty years and one block away from Silver Hawk automobile production, the South Bend White Sox changed their name to the South Bend Silver Hawks, paying tribute to this piece of South Bend history.

Not to Be Confused With: Lexington Studebakers

Between the Lines: The Silver Hawks installed artificial turf at Coveleski Stadium before the 2011 season to limit cancellations from early season rain and snow.

TERRE HAUTE HOTTENTOTS

League: Central League
City: Terre Haute, IN
Years: 1892, 1895, 1900-1909

1909 Terre Haute Hottentots
—National Baseball Hall of Fame Library.
Cooperstown, NY

The Terre Haute Hottentots shared the same nickname as an Indian Tribe with origins in South Africa. The name *Hottentot* translates to "stutterer" in Dutch, a description given to the speaking pattern of this tribe, mimicking the rhythmic manner in which they spoke. The Hottentots played in the Class B Central League, taking on teams like the Fort Wayne Billikens. Terre Haute, now known as the home of the Indiana State Sycamores, interestingly had a baseball team named the Terre Haute Hoosiers in 1888, the same nickname as Indiana State's rival University of Indiana.

Not to Be Confused With: Memphis Chickasaws, Lynn Papooses

Between the Lines: Mordecai "Three Finger" Brown made his professional debut for the Hottentots against the Rockford Red Sox on May 1, 1901. Brown would go on to pitch 14 seasons in the Major Leagues and was inducted into the National Baseball Hall of Fame in 1949.

Iowa

CLINTON LUMBERKINGS

League: Midwest League
City: Clinton, IA
Years: 1994-Present

Clinton baseball fan Norma Stauffer heard the Clinton Giants wanted a new team name in 1994 to create their own identity. She spent days and nights in the fall of 1993 pondering the best submission. Her father worked for Curtis Company, one of numerous lumber corporations in Clinton, and she thought the team name should honor the dependable lumber workers in the area. She suggested LumberKings and won season tickets, $100 cash, a team cap and a team jacket.

Not to Be Confused With: Oakdale Lumberjacks

Between the Lines: The LumberKings hosted baseball's first sudden-death "bunt-off" the day before the 2009 Midwest League All-Star Game. Great Lakes Loons shortstop Dee Gordon was the top bunter. They also held a Home Run Derby.

DES MOINES UNDERTAKERS

League: Western League
City: Des Moines, IA
Years: 1903

CLARK, COLUMBUS

Josh Clarke played for the Des Moines Undertakers in 1903
—Library of Congress photo (Name on card spelled incorrectly).

The Des Moines Undertakers broke ground in 1903, in the middle of a string of nickname changes for Des Moines professional baseball. In a span of seven seasons, fans cheered for the Des Moines Midgets, Des Moines Undertakers, Des Moines Prohibitionists, Des Moines Underwriters, Des Moines Champions, Des Moines Champs and Des Moines Boosters. The Boosters name stuck the longest during this era, holding the label from 1908 until 1925, when the nickname was haunted and replaced by the Des Moines Demons.

Not to Be Confused With: Americus Pall Bearers

Between the Lines: Des Moines hosted the first night baseball game under permanent lights in 1930. The game versus Wichita drew 12,000 fans.

MUSCATINE BUTTONMAKERS

League: Central Association
City: Muscatine, IA
Years: 1914

The Muscatine Buttonmakers took the field the same year Muscatine, Iowa, was proclaimed "The Pearl Button Capital of the United States." Residents in this city discovered pearls in the nearby Mississippi River, and dozens of button factories soon followed. Today you can eat at the Button Factory Restaurant in Muscatine after a day spent at the Muscatine Pearl Button Museum.

Not to Be Confused With: Canton Watchmakers

Between the Lines: Today, Cliff Lee is considered one of the best pitchers in Major League Baseball, but the Buttonmakers had a Cliff Lee of their own. The right hander was a position player for the 1914 Buttonmakers before becoming a pitcher and stuck in the Major Leagues for eight seasons.

SIOUX CITY EXPLORERS

League: American Association
City: Sioux City, IA
Years: 1993-Present

Lewis and Clark Park—home of the Sioux City Explorers
—Courtesy of Brian Merzbach

The Sioux City Explorers professional baseball team is named after two of the most famous explorers in American history, Lewis and Clark. Sioux City is a city in northeast Iowa, right along the Missouri River, and the city is still filled with brands from the Lewis and Clark journey. The Explorers play at Lewis and Clark Park, a few miles away from the Sioux City Lewis and Clark Interpretive Center.

Not to Be Confused With: Springfield Foot Trackers, Decatur Nomads, Elmira Pioneers

Between the Lines: It may not be Yankees vs. Red Sox, but the Explorers have a heated rival of their own, playing the Sioux Falls Fighting Pheasants each summer in the "I-29 Series."

HUTCHINSON SALT PACKERS

League: Western League
City: Hutchinson, KS
Years: 1906, 1908-1911, 1918

1910 Hutchinson Salt Packers
—National Baseball Hall of Fame Library.
Cooperstown, NY

The Hutchinson Salt Packers added some flavor to the Class C Western Association in 1908. Hutchinson is known as "The Salt City," and is still home to an active underground salt museum. Carey Salt Company is based in Hutchinson, and Cargill and Morton Salt also have plants there. Other professional baseball team names in Hutchinson have included the Hutchinson Salt Miners, Hutchinson Wheat Shockers and Hutchinson Larks.

Not to Be Confused With: New Iberia Sugar Boys

Between the Lines: The Salt Packers disbanded at the end of the 1918 season as a result of World War I. Many minor league clubs did the same because a high volume of players joined the Armed Forces.

IOLA GASBAGS

League: Missouri Valley League
City: Iola, KS
Years: 1902, 1904

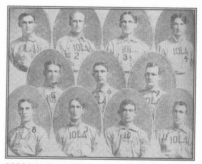

1904 Iola Gasbags
—National Baseball Hall of Fame Library.
Cooperstown, NY

The Iola Gasbags didn't have much to be boastful about in 1902, finishing 52 games out of first place in the Missouri Valley League. The Class D circuit also featured the Joplin Miners and Sedalia Gold Bugs that year. By 1903, Iola's team was being called the Gaslighters. The city of 6,000 people in Kansas has had their share of baseball team nicknames, like the Iola Grays, Iola Champs and Iola Indians.

Not to Be Confused With: Sydney Mines Ramblers, Lumberton Auctioneers

Between the Lines: Iola was an early stop in the wandering career of Herman Meek, who played 17 seasons in the minor leagues for over 15 teams in the early 1900s. For his journey, Meek later gained the nickname "Dad."

KANSAS CITY T-BONES

League: Northern League
City: Kansas City, KS
Years: 2003-Present

Everything surrounding the Kansas City T-Bones is an allusion to the meat history in Kansas City. In addition to the team name being a type of steak, fans can shop at the Meat Locker Team Store, sign up to join the Lil Chops Kids Club, where upon joining, you get a birthday card from the T-Bones official mascot Sizzle. Kansas City's association with steak started with the Kansas City Stockyards in 1871.

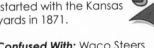

Not to Be Confused With: Waco Steers

Between the Lines: The T-Bones had a fitting giveaway item for fans on June 2, 2011, handing out free cowbells. The cowbells were provided by the Midwest Dairy Association.

LEAVENWORTH CONVICTS

League: Western Association
City: Leavenworth, KS
Years: 1907

Leavenworth Convicts
—National Baseball Hall of Fame Library. Cooperstown, NY

The Leavenworth Convicts took their name from the most well-known piece of this city, Leavenworth Federal Prison. The facility has brought some of the most high-profile criminals to Kansas since it opened in 1895. On the field, there was no parole for the last place Convicts in 1907. They finished behind the Webb City Goldbugs, Wichita Jobbers and the rest of the Class C Western Association. Other parts of Leavenworth's history have persuaded team nicknames as well. Fort Leavenworth was the inspiration for the Leavenworth Soldiers team name in the 1880s.

Not to Be Confused With: Crookston Crooks

Between the Lines: The Convicts were imprisoned by the pitching of C.H. Clark on May 20, 1907, as the Wichita Jobbers hurler threw a no-hitter against Leavenworth.

TOPEKA SAVAGES

League: Western League
City: Topeka, KS
Years: 1916

In a battle between nine savages and nine wolves, who would win? Fans of the Class A Western League asked this question in 1916 every time the Topeka Savages took on the in-state rival Wichita Wolves. Topeka's professional baseball team was called the Savages for just the 1916 season. The Kansas capital city had other unique team nicknames during its time in the Western League, like the Topeka Capitals, Topeka Populists and Topeka Golden Giants.

Joe Agler played for the 1916 Topeka Savages
—Library of Congress photo

Not to Be Confused With: Bakersfield Outlaws

Between the Lines: Many consider Cy Young the greatest pitcher in history, but Cy Lambert was the greatest pitcher on June 26, 1916. Lambert threw a no-hitter for the Savages against the St. Joseph Drummers.

WICHITA IZZIES

League: Western League
City: Wichita, KS
Years: 1923-1926

Minor league stadiums are often named after well-respected members of cities throughout America, but what about a team named after a beloved local? This was the case for the Wichita Izzies, named after Wichita, Kansas, legend Frank Isbell. A longtime minor leaguer in Wichita, Isbell would go on to be a civic leader in Wichita's city government. The Izzies played in the Class A Western League in the 1920s against teams like the Amarillo Texans and Sioux City Packers. Other team names in Wichita baseball history include the Wichita Witches and Wichita Wranglers.

Fred Beck played for the Wichita Izzies in 1924
—Library of Congress photo

Not to Be Confused With: Niagara Falls Citizens

Between the Lines: There were some messy scorebooks at the Izzies game on September 14, 1924. Wichita lost 16-15 in 15 innings to the Denver Bears that night.

WICHITA WINGNUTS

League: American Association
City: Wichita, KS
Years: 2008-Present

The Wichita Wingnuts team name has nothing to do with wings or nuts. The Wingnuts moniker is a playful nod to Wichita's place in aviation. The two largest employers in Wichita are both in the aircraft industry, Cessna Aircraft Company and Spirit AeroSystems. The first airplane built for commercial use was created in 1920 in Wichita, and at one time the city was referred to as "The Air Capital of the World."

Not to Be Confused With: Newark Co-Pilots, Montgomery Bombers

Between the Lines: The Wingnuts actually asked their fans to be silent for half of a game in June of 2011. The unique promotion came on the anniversary of when the Miranda Rights came into existence.

BOWLING GREEN HOT RODS

League: South Atlantic League
City: Bowling Green, KY
Years: 2009-Present

Bowling Green, Kentucky's first professional baseball team in over 65 years came out of the garage in style. The Bowling Green Hot Rods take their name from the region's car history, with the team playing a few miles away from the National Corvette Museum. The Hot Rods took their first test drive through the Single-A South Atlantic League in 2009. The franchise was previously in Georgia, swimming through the Sally League as the Columbus Catfish. Team management cruised through over 1,000 fan suggestions for the team name and narrowed the list of candidates to Bluegills, Cave Shrimp, Mammoths, Speedsters, Sparkplugs and Turbos before deciding on Hot Rods.

Not to Be Confused With: Pine Bluff Locomotives

Between the Lines: The name Cave Shrimp gathered such strong support in the team voting that the Hot Rods held "What Could've Been Night" at a 2009 game and handed out mock Bowling Green Cave Shrimp t-shirts to fans.

Kentucky

Louisiana

HOPKINSVILLE HOPPERS

League: Kitty League
City: Hopkinsville, KY
Years: 1905, 1910-1914, 1916, 1922-1923, 1935-1942, 1946-1954

The Hopkinsville Hoppers team nickname first appeared in 1910 in the Class D Kitty League. The team is not believed to be named after frogs or any other leaping creature but referred to the skipping city-to-city pace a minor league team endures throughout a season. The Kitty League has an interesting background to its name also. The league was originally dubbed the KIT League

1910 Hopkinsville Hoppers
—National Baseball Hall of Fame Library.
Cooperstown, NY

in 1903, short for the Kentucky-Illinois-Tennessee League. The KIT League became affectionately and then officially called the Kitty League in 1905.

Not to Be Confused With: Miller Jugglers

Between the Lines: The Hoppers 1905 season was shortened when the league shut down because of a yellow fever epidemic.

BATON ROUGE RED STICKS

League: Evangeline League
City: Baton Rouge, LA
Years: 1903-1904, 1934, 1946-1955

Three French explorers in 1699 wrote of a tall, blood-stained pole used to divide the territories of the Bayou Goula and Houma Indians. It is because of this red stick that the explorers named the newly discovered city *le Baton Rouge,* translating to "the red stick." The Baton Rouge Red Sticks

Alex Box Stadium—former home of the Baton Rouge Red Sticks
—Courtesy of Brian Merzbach

appeared in the Class D Evangeline League in 1947, finishing seventh while the Alexandria Aces and Hammond Berries moved on to the playoffs.

Not to Be Confused With: Paris Red Peppers, Lancaster Red Roses, Riverside Red Wave, Scranton/Wilkes-Barre Red Barons

Between the Lines: The Red Sticks encountered some interesting wildlife while playing road games in Gulf-based cities. Two Evangeline League umpires grabbed bats to take care of a cottonmouth moccasin snake that had slithered onto the field during a 1952 game.

NEW ORLEANS ZEPHYRS

League: Pacific Coast League
City: New Orleans, LA
Years: 1993-Present

A zephyr is a type of wind, but this team nickname has nothing to do with the infamously stormy weather in New Orleans. In fact, the franchise was nicknamed the Zephyrs even before it played in New Orleans. After the 1992 season, the Denver Zephyrs of the Triple-A American Association moved to New Orleans, a move prompted by the expansion of the Colorado Rockies into the National League. The team was originally named after the Denver *Zephyr*, a passenger train connecting Chicago and Denver.

Not to Be Confused With: Jonesboro Zebras

Between the Lines: On April 6, 2006, an emotional crowd of over 11,000 people filled Zephyr Field for the first outdoor sporting event in New Orleans since Hurricane Katrina seven months before.

OPELOUSAS ORPHANS

League: Cotton States League
City: Opelousas, LA
Years: 1932

No, the Opelousas Orphans were not a team abandoned by their manager. Opelousas, Louisiana, was a stop for the Orphan Trains beginning in 1907, when children from overpopulated orphanages were relocated to more rural areas. The City of Opelousas is in the process of building an Orphan Train Museum. One Orphans opponent in the Class D Cotton States League also had a childish name, the Monroe Twins.

Not to Be Confused With: Quincy Infants

Between the Lines: The Orphans player/manager Milt Delmas played for the Brooklyn Dodgers in 1933.

Maine

BANGOR BLUE OX

League: Northeast League
City: Bangor, ME
Years: 1996-1997

In downtown Bangor, Maine, there stands a statue built of Paul Bunyan. Playing off Bunyan's legend in the community, the local professional baseball team was named the Blue Ox, after Bunyan's loyal ox Babe. The Blue Ox left central Maine after the 1997 season, finishing last

Mahaney Diamond— former home of the Bangor Blue Ox —Courtesy of Brian Merzbach

behind the Massachusetts Mad Dogs, Adirondack Lumberjacks and others. The Blue Ox inaugural team had a player with a unique nickname himself, Oil Can Boyd. The former Major League pitcher went 10-0 for Bangor in 1996.

Not to Be Confused With: Lakewood BlueClaws, Memphis Blues

Between the Lines: With Boyd's perfect record and 35-year-old Mike Smith's 1.15 ERA, the Blue Ox pitching staff found the fountain of youth.

LEWISTON CUPIDS

League: New England League
City: Lewiston, ME
Years: 1914-1915

Pitchers and catchers report to spring training each year in mid-February, but the Lewiston Cupids stayed in the Valentine's Day mood all season. The Cupids aimed their arrows at opponents like the Fitchburg Burghers, Lynn Fighters and Portland Duffs. The Cupids never had a winning season in the Class B New England League, and a few years later the local team was called the Lewiston-Auburn Twins.

Not to Be Confused With: Palatka Azaleas, Victoria Rosebuds

Joe Judge played for the Lewiston Cupids in 1914
—Library of Congress photo

Between the Lines: The best player in Cupids history was Joe Judge. He went on to play 20 seasons in the Major Leagues and accumulate 2,352 hits in the Deadball Era. Judge hit two of the Washington Senators' four home runs in 1917.

ABERDEEN IRONBIRDS

League: New York-Penn League
City: Aberdeen, MD
Years: 2002-Present

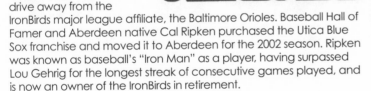

The Aberdeen IronBirds team nickname combines references to the squad's parent club and team owner. The IronBirds play at Ripken Stadium in Aberdeen, Maryland, just a 45-minute drive away from the IronBirds major league affiliate, the Baltimore Orioles. Baseball Hall of Famer and Aberdeen native Cal Ripken purchased the Utica Blue Sox franchise and moved it to Aberdeen for the 2002 season. Ripken was known as baseball's "Iron Man" as a player, having surpassed Lou Gehrig for the longest streak of consecutive games played, and is now an owner of the IronBirds in retirement.

Not to Be Confused With: Delmarva Shorebirds, Crowley Rice Birds

Between the Lines: The first pitch in IronBirds history ended up over the fence. Ryan Keefer threw the pitch that Domingo Cuello whacked over the outfield wall, helping the Williamsport Crosscutters spoil Aberdeen's Opening Night.

FREDERICK KEYS

League: Carolina League
City: Frederick, MD
Years: 1989-Present

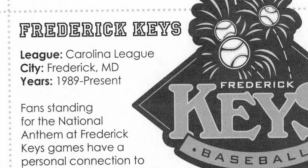

Fans standing for the National Anthem at Frederick Keys games have a personal connection to this team nickname. The Keys are named after Francis Scott Key, the poet who wrote the *Star Spangled Banner*, and native of Frederick County, Maryland. The Keys regularly promote their musical background and even named their team mascot Keynote. The Keys joined the Single-A Carolina League in 1989, finishing in first place ahead of the likes of the Salem Buccaneers and Winston-Salem Spirits.

Not to Be Confused With: Burlington Bees

Between the Lines: For one night in 1998, it felt like the Keys were named after their starting pitcher. Major League All-Star Jimmy Key pitched for Frederick on an injury rehab assignment, throwing six innings and picking up the win.

HAGERSTOWN HUBS

League: Blue Ridge League
City: Hagerstown, MD
Years: 1924-1931

Municipal Stadium—Hagerstown, MD
—Courtesy of Hagerstown Suns

Hagerstown is known as the "Hub City," and the Hagerstown Hubs took their nickname after the city nickname. Hagerstown originally earned the title of "Hub City" because of the number of major railroads passing through it. The anchor of the Western Maryland Railway, Hagerstown also served as a point on the Baltimore and Ohio, Norfolk and Western, and Pennsylvania railroads. Hagerstown has had a lengthy roster of team names to play at Municipal Stadium over the years, including the Hagerstown Blues, Hagerstown Owls, Hagerstown Packets, Hagerstown Terriers and Hagerstown Suns.

Not to Be Confused With: Lubbock Hubbers

Between the Lines: Minor leagues used to host post-season interleague play. The Hubs defeated the Cambridge Canners to win the Five-State Championship in 1925.

BROCKTON SHOEMAKERS

League: New England League
City: Brockton, MA
Years: 1893-1899, 1910-1914, 1928-1929

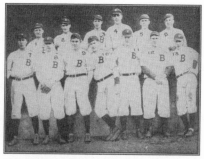

1910 Brockton Shoemakers
—National Baseball Hall of Fame Library.
Cooperstown, NY

Brockton was known as the center for shoe making in Massachusetts throughout the 1800s. With similar factories in nearby Lynn and Haverhill, shoe making was the prime occupation in the area for decades. With shoe production so closely tied to Brockton, the city's entry in the New England League became known as the Brockton Shoemakers. Today the Brockton City Historical Society invites visitors to "the only authentic Shoe Museum in America."

Not to Be Confused With: Mayfield Pantmakers, Holland Wooden Shoes

Between the Lines: Brockton is only a half-hour from Boston, and Shoemakers pitcher Fred Anderson became a local legend when he was called up by the defending World Series champion Red Sox during his stellar 1913 season in Brockton.

HOLYOKE PAPERWEIGHTS

League: Connecticut League
City: Holyoke, MA
Years: 1903-1906

Paper production in Holyoke, Massachusetts, was so overwhelming that the city apparently needed their baseball team's name to control it. The 1800s were a growing time for Holyoke, when dozens of water-powered paper mills were reviving the city. One result of this paper mill boom was American Pad and Paper Company, still a profitable office supply producer today. Trying to weigh down the Springfield Ponies and New London Whalers, the Holyoke Paperweights won the Class D Connecticut League in 1903.

1906 Holyoke Paperweights
—National Baseball Hall of Fame Library.
Cooperstown, NY

Not to Be Confused With: Greenville Staplers

Between the Lines: New York Yankees pitcher C.C. Sabathia signed a $161 million contract before the 2009 season, but another C.C. was paid far less a century before. Paperweights pitcher C.C. Hodge's contract was purchased for 25 cents in 1906.

SALEM WITCHES

League: New England League
City: Salem, MA
Years: 1888, 1926-1928, 1930

The Salem Witches modeled their team name after the most famous events ever to take place in Salem, Massachusetts. The Salem Witch Museum still describes the events of 1692 and 1693, when some area residents were accused of witchcraft. These accusations resulted in the Salem witch trials, and 19 of the people found guilty were hanged. By 1888 the Salem Witches appeared in the New England League standings, and the team kept the mystical name for decades to come, spooking the Haverhill Hillies, Portland Eskimos, Attleboro Burros and Nashua Millionaires.

Stuffy McInnis managed the Salem Witches in 1928
—Library of Congress photo

Not to Be Confused With: Dayton Dragons, Frostburg Demons, Minot Magicians

Between the Lines: The 1926 Witches did not start in Salem. After a 6-8 record and some business struggles as the Lowell Highwaymen, manager Tom "Poke" Whalen moved the franchise to Salem at midseason.

WORCESTER TORNADOES

League: Can-Am League
City: Worcester, MA
Years: 2005-Present

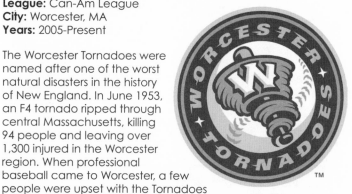

The Worcester Tornadoes were named after one of the worst natural disasters in the history of New England. In June 1953, an F4 tornado ripped through central Massachusetts, killing 94 people and leaving over 1,300 injured in the Worcester region. When professional baseball came to Worcester, a few people were upset with the Tornadoes team name, feeling the devastating tornado was still fresh in the minds of some older residents. More recently, in games against the likes of the Atlantic City Surf, New Haven County Cutters and North Shore Spirit, fans have been entertained by the official team mascot Twister.

Not to Be Confused With: Brooklyn Cyclones

Between the Lines: The Tornadoes play on a field steeped in history. Fitton Field opened in 1905 and Lou Gehrig, Babe Ruth and Ted Williams have all played there.

KALAMAZOO CELERY PICKERS

League: Central League
City: Kalamazoo, MI
Years: 1920-1923, 1926

The Kalamazoo Celery Pickers played a few miles from where Cornelius De Bruin first planted celery seeds on the banks of the Kalamazoo River. Within a few years, celery fields were blossoming in southwest Michigan and Kalamazoo was being called "Celery City." The Celery Pickers played in the Class B Central League, trying to grow past the Muskegon Muskies and Ionia Mayors.

Not to Be Confused With: Saskatoon Berrypickers, Greenville Cotton Pickers, Porterville Orange Pickers

Between the Lines: Horace Browne threw a no-hitter for the Celery Pickers on August 4, 1923 against the Grand Rapids Billbobs.

Boss Schmidt managed the 1920 Kalamazoo Celery Pickers
—Library of Congress photo

KALAMAZOO KAZOOS

League: Ohio State League
City: Kalamazoo, MI
Years: 1887-1889, 1909-1910, 1913-1914, 1924

The Kalamazoo Kazoos were music to their fans' ears in 1887, finishing atop the nine-team Ohio State League in their inaugural year. Led by skipper Al Buckenberger (it seems fitting that the Kalamazoo Kazoos manager would have an eccentric name), the Kazoos beat teams like the Zanesville Kickapoos

1909 Kalamazoo Kazoos
—National Baseball Hall of Fame Library. Cooperstown, NY

that year. The buzzing musical instrument was first brought to the United States in Macon, Georgia. This team took their name only because of the verbal similarities between Kalamazoo and Kazoo.

Not to Be Confused With: Sioux City Soos

Between the Lines: Former Kazoos pitcher Hal Elliott appeared in the most National League games (48) in 1930.

LANSING LUGNUTS

League: Midwest League
City: Lansing, MI
Years: 1995-Present

The Lansing Lugnuts team name initially sparked a stalled response. When the team moved to Michigan in 1995 and changed its name, the local automotive industry was a sensitive subject because General Motors and Chrysler were moving jobs out of the area. Before their first Midwest League season, the *Lansing State Journal* took a poll on the approval rating of the new Lugnuts team name. The results came back, and over 90 percent of voters checked "strongly disliked" for their feelings on Lugnuts. Lansing has grown to identify with the name Lugnuts, and these days fans chant the official team slogan of "Go Nuts" while at Oldsmobile Park.

Not to Be Confused With: Portsmouth Truckers

Between the Lines: On Easter Sunday in 2003, three Lugnuts pitchers combined to throw a no-hitter against Dayton. In the same game, Donnie Hood hit for the cycle. It is believed to be the only time in professional baseball that the same team accomplished both feats on the same day.

MICHIGAN BATTLE CATS

League: Midwest League
City: Battle Creek, MI
Years: 1995-2002

C.O. Brown Stadium—former home of the Michigan Battle Cats
—Courtesy of Brian Merzbach

When the Michigan Battle Cats first moved to southwest Michigan in 1995, the original moniker was "Golden Kazoos" to tie in with nearby Kalamazoo, Michigan. After a local clash between cities Kalamazoo and Battle Creek, Michigan, over which city owned the rights to the team name, team owners appeased both cities and renamed the team Michigan Battle Cats, without ever playing a game as the Golden Kazoos. The Battle Cats took on Midwest League rivals like the West Michigan Whitecaps before changing affiliates and team names in 2002, becoming the Battle Creek Yankees.

Not to Be Confused With: Gary-Southshore RailCats

Between the Lines: The 1999 Battle Cats pitching staff made Midwest League hitters want to call in sick. Johan Santana and Roy Oswalt were in the same Single-A rotation that year. The pair combined to strike out over 3,500 Major League batters.

MT. CLEMENS BATHERS

League: Southern Michigan League
City: Mt. Clemens, MI
Years: 1906-1907, 1912-1914

1907 Mt. Clemens Bathers
—National Baseball Hall of Fame Library. Cooperstown, NY

One of the cleanest teams in Minor League Baseball history, the Mt. Clemens Bathers used their name as a salute to the mineral bath industry in Mt. Clemens, Michigan. The city had scattered mineral bath sites bringing in travelers from across the country to take advantage of the healing effects indoor mineral baths provided. The Mt. Clemens Bathers first appeared in the Class D Southern Michigan League, but they didn't exactly make a splash, finishing last among teams like the Battle Creek Crickets and Jackson Convicts.

Not to Be Confused With: Niagara Falls Rapids

Between the Lines: The Bathers pitching staff was unhittable in August 1912. Thomas Caesar threw a no-hitter against Wyandotte on August 14, and two days later his Bathers teammate Lou North threw a no-hitter too!

Minnesota

DULUTH WHALEBACKS

League: Western Association
City: Duluth, MN
Years: 1891

There are no whales in Minnesota. The Duluth Whalebacks took their name after a ship created in the upper Midwest called the *Whaleback Steamer*. Captain Alexander McDougall designed the steamboat with a cylinder-shaped body for more effective cargo shipment throughout the Great Lakes. McDougall built the first Whaleback in Duluth in 1888, and three years later the Duluth Whalebacks' team name honored his contribution to shipbuilding.

Not to Be Confused With:
Tarboro Serpents

Between the Lines: With a name like Scrappy Carroll, you'd have to be a fan favorite, and Carroll was for the 1891 Whalebacks. Fans were delighted to see Carroll's effort even after proving himself in the Major Leagues for three seasons in the 1880s.

Charlie Sprague played for the Duluth Whalebacks in 1891
—Library of Congress photo

VIRGINIA ORE DIGGERS

League: Northern League
City: Virginia, MN
Years: 1913-1916

The Virginia Ore Diggers didn't play in the Virginia you're picturing. The Ore Diggers shoveled through the Class C Northern League in Virginia, Minnesota. The city of Virginia is set on the Mesabi Iron Range and is within Minnesota's Iron Range, where iron ore mining is still a significant part of the community and provides many jobs.

Not to Be Confused With: Fort Scott Hay Diggers, Seattle Clamdiggers

Between the Lines: Rube Waddell's Hall of Fame career in the Major Leagues ended in 1910, but he continued his career with the Ore Diggers in 1913. Fans were dazzled to see the great southpaw pitch a 12-inning game against the Duluth White Sox that season.

Hall of Famer Rube Waddell played for the Virginia Ore Diggers in 1913
—Library of Congress photo

VICKSBURG HILL BILLIES

League: Cotton States League
City: Vicksburg, MS
Years: 1903-1907, 1910-1912, 1922-1932, 1937, 1941, 1950, 1955

The Vicksburg Hill Billies team name did not have the connotation in the early 1900s that it does today. The phrase originally referred to people living on a hill, which applies to Vicksburg, Mississippi. Part of the city is set on a high bluff overlooking the Mississippi River. The Vicksburg Hill Billies tried to stay above teams like the Jackson Drummers and Greenwood Chauffeurs in the Class D Cotton States League.

1928 Vicksburg Hill Billies
—National Baseball Hall of Fame Library.
Cooperstown, NY

Not to Be Confused With: Lynchburg Hillcats, Ozark Mountain Ducks

Between the Lines: The Hill Billies tested their fans' patience on July 11, 1904, when they played the Greenville Cotton Pickers for 20 innings before eventually settling on a 2-2 tie.

YAZOO CITY ZOOS

League: Delta League
City: Yazoo City, MS
Years: 1904, 1910-1912

The New York Yankees were once jokingly called the "Bronx Zoo" because of the chaos surrounding the team, but as far as we know this group of Zoos was relatively calm. The Zoos team name was a shortened version

1911 Yazoo City Zoos
—National Baseball Hall of Fame Library.
Cooperstown, NY

of their city's name, Yazoo City, Mississippi. The Yazoo City Zoos played their games a few miles from the Yazoo River, the river that Yazoo City is named after.

Not to Be Confused With: Alexandria Hoo Hoos

Between the Lines: A Zoos catcher with the last name of Taylor caught for both teams during a doubleheader on June 11, 1912. The Columbus Joy Riders catcher was injured early in the first game of the twin bill, and Taylor volunteered to stay behind the plate for both the Zoos and the Joy Riders.

Missouri

HANNIBAL CANNIBALS

League: Illinois-Missouri League
City: Hannibal, MO
Years: 1908-1912

Clemens Field— former home of the Hannibal Cannibals
—Courtesy of Brian Merzbach

The Hannibal Cannibals team name probably had fans wondering what players ate to get ready for a game. This nickname was not solely for intimidation though; it actually had a local literary twist. Author Samuel Clemens was from Hannibal, Missouri, and the Cannibals team name was a reference to his short story "Cannibalism in the Cars," written under the pen name Mark Twain. The stadium in Hannibal was named after Clemens and stands to this day. The Cannibals moved on to the Class D Central Association in 1909, trying to cut through the Burlington Pathfinders, Kewanee Boilermakers, Ottumwa Speedboys and Muscatine Camels.

Not to Be Confused With: Terrell Terrors

Between the Lines: Outfielder Dan Kerwin played in two Major League games for the 1903 Cincinnati Reds, and then played nine more seasons in the minor leagues trying to get back, joining the Cannibals for the 1910 season. He never played in another big league game.

KIRKSVILLE OSTEOPATHS

League: Missouri State League
City: Kirksville, MO
Years: 1911

There may be no team in less of a need for a trainer than the Kirksville Osteopaths. Kirksville is where osteopathic medicine was invented, and the city is still home to the Kirksville College of Osteopathic Medicine at A.T. Still University. Still founded what was then called the American School of Osteopathy in 1892. The Kirksville Osteopaths played just one season, finishing fourth in the five-team Class D Missouri State League, only medicating past the last place Brookfield Hustlers.

Not to Be Confused With: Arkansas City Osages

Between the Lines: Osteopaths slugger David Kraft was the Missouri State League home run champion in 1911. He hit three.

NEVADA LUNATICS

League: Missouri Valley League
City: Nevada, MO
Years: 1902-1903

Before you picture a crazed gambler, we should point out the Nevada Lunatics played in Nevada, Missouri—nowhere near Las Vegas. Nevada (pronounced Nuh-VAY-duh) was the site of the Nevada State Hospital, a mental institution near the Missouri and Kansas border. In the early 1900s, the Nevada State Hospital was also referred to as the lunatic asylum, and that is how the Lunatics took their name.

Not to Be Confused With: La Crosse Outcasts

Between the Lines: In the two years of their existence, the Lunatics sent two players to the Major Leagues. One of the players, Harry Cheek, came to bat over 5,000 times in the minor leagues and earned his place in history with four Major League at bats for the Philadelphia Phillies in 1910.

BUTTE SMOKE EATERS

League: Montana State League
City: Butte, MT
Years: 1900

Butte's entry in the Montana State League made light of the biggest natural concern in the Treasure State—wildfires. The Smoke Eaters played in the Montana State League, a circuit featuring the Helena Senators and Anaconda Serpents. Exactly 100 years after the Smoke Eaters first and only season, it was the Butte Copper Kings of the Pioneer League eating smoke, as a few of their games were "smoked out" that season due to wildfires in western Montana.

Not to Be Confused With: St. Joseph Clay Eaters

Between the Lines: In the early 1900s it was fairly common for managers to also play for the team they were running. Jim Powell, the 40-year-old player/manager of the Smoke Eaters in 1900, was 23 years older than Butte pitcher Jim St. Vrain.

Dad Clarke played for the Butte Smoke Eaters in 1900
—Library of Congress photo

GREAT FALLS VOYAGERS

League: Pioneer League
City: Great Falls, MT
Years: 2008-Present

PBL trademarks and copyrights are used under license

In 1950, Great Falls Electrics General Manager Nick Mariana was in his office at Legion Park when he spotted silver flying saucers above the baseball stadium. Mariana grabbed a video camera to capture the bright, distant objects, introducing America to the now infamous "Mariana UFO Incident." While the Great Falls Voyagers team name pays tribute to Mariana's crafty camera work, Mariana himself was in charge of a team with a unique name on that day in 1950: the Great Falls Electrics. Great Falls is known as the "Electric City," with hydroelectric dams in Great Falls built along the banks of the Missouri River.

Not to Be Confused With: Huntsville Stars

Between the Lines: Voyagers fans received a unique giveaway item on June 24, 2011, when Ace Hardware handed out wooden nickels to fans entering the ballpark.

BEATRICE MILKSKIMMERS

League: Nebraska State League
City: Beatrice, NE
Years: 1913-1915

1914 Beatrice Milkskimmers
—National Baseball Hall of Fame Library.
Cooperstown, NY

The Beatrice Milkskimmers had a sour first season, falling behind rivals like the Superior Brickmakers and Fremont Pathfinders in their inaugural year. In milk processing plants, a separator divides heavier milk fat from the lighter milk to create skim milk. In the early 1900s, when dairy farms and processing plants were a main source of employment in southern Nebraska, naming the team after the milk skimming process seemed appropriate.

Not to Be Confused With: Racine Malted Milks

Between the Lines: For a team that only existed three years, the Milkskimmers had some dramatic moments. Frank McDermott threw a no-hitter against the York Prohibitionists in 1914, and a year later the club won the Nebraska State League.

LINCOLN TREE PLANTERS

League: Western League
City: Lincoln, NE
Years: 1886-1888

The lack of trees in Nebraska's terrain indirectly led to the Lincoln Tree Planters team name. J. Sterling Morton was one of the first pioneers to move into the Nebraska Territory in the 1850s, and one of his first goals was to plant more trees for agricultural and visual reasons. Morton later created Arbor Day, a tree planting holiday still active today, and Nebraska became known for its dedication to planting trees.

Not to Be Confused With: Grays Harbor Loggers, Missoula Timberjacks

Between the Lines: The Tree Planters had dozens of successful players, but none more uniquely named than Icicle Reeder, who played for the Washington Nationals and Cincinnati Red Stockings in the Major Leagues.

Hall of Famer Jake Beckley played for the Lincoln Tree Planters in 1887
—Library of Congress photo

OMAHA GOLDEN SPIKES

League: Pacific Coast League
City: Omaha, NE
Years: 1999-2001

Omaha is the pinnacle of the college baseball world, and the award given to the best college baseball player each year is called the Golden Spikes Award, but surprisingly, the Omaha Golden Spikes team name actually chronicles back to railroad history and has nothing to do with

Rosenblatt Stadium—former home of the Omaha Golden Spikes
—Courtesy of Omaha Royals

the college baseball connection. When the first Transcontinental Railroad was completed in May 1869, a ceremonial golden spike was hammered into the ground in Promontory Summit, Utah. The Transcontinental Railroad started in Omaha and eventually reached Sacramento.

Not to Be Confused With: State College Spikes, Ogden Spikers

Between the Lines: The Golden Spikes 2000 roster featured two future Major League All-Stars—Carlos Beltran and Lance Carter.

OMAHA STORM CHASERS

League: Pacific Coast League
City: Omaha, NE
Years: 2011-Present

The longstanding Triple-A affiliate of the Kansas City Royals wanted a new team name to coincide with the team's move to a new stadium in 2011. The name-the-team vote presented 24 semi-finalists, by far the most choices fans have had anywhere in recent selection processes. In the end, Storm Chasers was unveiled along with the new team mascots Stormy and Vortex. The name recognizes the extreme weather Nebraskans see throughout the year. It also "pokes a little fun at the variety of weather we experience here," said team President Martie Cordaro at the time of the announcement.

Not to Be Confused With: Cooleemee Cools

Between the Lines: As if opening a stunning ballpark with a new brand wasn't enough, the Storm Chasers won the Pacific Coast League Championship in 2011.

LAS VEGAS 51S

League: Pacific Coast League
City: Las Vegas, NV
Years: 2001-Present

The Las Vegas 51s team name makes you think the signs from their third base coach may be extra secretive. The 51s name originates from Area 51, the highly restricted military base in southern Nevada. Area 51 is a central point in many UFO and alien conspiracies, something the ball club references with its logo showing a gray alien with baseball seams on its head.

Not to Be Confused With: Inland Empire 66ers

Between the Lines: An afternoon Easter egg hunt for kids went awry in 1993 in Las Vegas. Over 2,000 pounds of chocolate melted on the grass, leaving brown stains on Cashman Field for the game vs. Sacramento that day.

MANCHESTER TEXTILES

League: New England League
City: Manchester, NH
Years: 1906, 1914-1915

The textile industry in Manchester dates back to the early 1800s, and the name of the city's professional baseball team, the Manchester Textiles, reflected the fabric of the community. Cotton spinning mills became a major employer in Manchester, getting their power from the nearby Merrimack River. Along with opponents like the Haverhill Hustlers, Worcester Busters and Lynn Shoemakers, the Textiles tried to sew up the Class B New England League against a team in a city with lots of cloth history themselves—the Lowell Tigers.

Pat Kilhullen played for the Manchester Textiles in 1914
—Library of Congress photo

Not to Be Confused With: Paterson Silk Weavers, Elkin Blanketeers

Between the Lines: Red Torphy played for Manchester for two seasons and later reached the Major Leagues with the Boston Braves.

NEW HAMPSHIRE FISHER CATS

League: Eastern League
City: Manchester, NH
Years: 2004-Present

The New Hampshire Fisher Cats ended up being the nickname to be named later. The franchise was originally named the New Hampshire Primaries, referencing the New Hampshire Presidential Primary. The backlash from the media and the public was so severe that management nixed the Primaries name before the team ever played a game. The New Hampshire Fisher Cats was selected as the new name and fans responded much better to the fast-running weasel.

Not to Be Confused With: Fort Worth Cats, Sacramento River Cats

Between the Lines: Before reaching the Major Leagues with the Toronto Blue Jays, Kyle Drabek threw a no-hitter for the Fisher Cats on July 4, 2010 in front of a sold-out crowd.

New Jersey

JERSEY CITY SKEETERS

League: Eastern League
City: Jersey City, NJ
Years: 1885, 1887-1889, 1902-1915, 1918-1933

The word "skeeters" is a shortened phrase referring to mosquitoes, and with the Jersey City Skeeters playing right near the Hudson River this team nickname became suitable. The Skeeters bit the rest of the Class A Eastern League in 1903,

1912 Jersey City Skeeters
— National Baseball Hall of Fame Library, Cooperstown, NY

winning their first 18 games of the season, becoming an itch to the Newark Sailors and Worcester Riddlers.

Not to Be Confused With: Berlin Busy Bees, Salt Lake Buzz

Between the Lines: Skeeters pitcher John Frill tossed a perfect game against the Providence Grays on July 6, 1912. The game was shortened, ending early because the two clubs agreed to let the umpire catch a train.

New Mexico

ALBUQUERQUE ISOTOPES

League: Pacific Coast League
City: Albuquerque, NM
Years: 2003-Present

There are many nuclear technology facilities in New Mexico, but the origination behind the Albuquerque Isotopes team name is a lot more animated. In an episode of "The Simpsons," Springfield goes into unrest when residents find out the Springfield Isotopes baseball team is moving to Albuquerque. Years after the episode aired, the Isotopes went from fiction to reality, when Isotopes won a name the team vote before the inaugural 2003 season. Now fans of the "Topes" can interact with the mascot Orbit, who is officially classified as "One Big Fuzzy Electron."

Not to Be Confused With:
Tri-City Atoms

Between the Lines: Larry Trujillo has won a car at an Isotopes game—twice. Trujillo won a contest giving away a car if an Isotopes player hit a grand slam. Nine months later, he entered the raffle at another game, another grand slam went over the fence, and his name was drawn again!

New Mexico

New York

ROSWELL ROCKETS

League: Longhorn League
City: Roswell, NM
Years: 1949-1956

Two summers after the famous Roswell UFO incident in 1947, the Roswell Rockets were searching for debris of victory in the Class D Longhorn League. The Rockets played 75 miles away from the crashing of materials some believe to be pieces of an alien aircraft. Roswell's team in years before the incident went by a less indigenous nickname, the Roswell Sunshiners.

Not to Be Confused With: Syracuse SkyChiefs

Between the Lines: Rockets slugger Joe Bauman set the Minor League Baseball single-season home run record in 1954, hitting 72 round trippers. The trophy given to the top home run hitter in Minor League Baseball today is called the Joe Bauman Award.

AUBURN PRISONERS

League: New York State League
City: Auburn, NY
Years: 1899

The Auburn Prisoners took the field a few cells away from the Auburn Prison, New York's first state penitentiary. The Prisoners began play in the New York State League in 1899, taking on teams with more peaceful nicknames like the Cortland Wagonmakers. Their debut season didn't live up to the intensity of their nickname, only finishing ahead of the Schenectady Electricians, and ending nine games behind the Albany Senators for sixth place.

Not to Be Confused With: Jefferson City Convicts

Between the Lines: The Prisoners relocated for the 1900 season and became the Troy Washerwomen. They had much better results there, producing Major Leaguers like John Atz and Tom Donovan.

BATAVIA MUCKDOGS

League: New York-Penn League
City: Batavia, NY
Years: 1998-Present

Digging their way past teams like the Mahoning Valley Scrappers, the Batavia Muckdogs garner more questions about their team name than any other in the New York-Penn League. Muck soil is a very fertile form of soil found in swampland areas of western New York. Muckdogs management attached the name "dogs" to the backside of this nickname, adding more life to the name, instead of basing it on dirt alone.

Not to Be Confused With: Moose Jaw Diamond Dogs, Charleston RiverDogs, Phoenix Desert Dogs

Between the Lines: A game between the Olean Oilers and Batavia had a skunk delay in 1951. Neither team was willing to chase the skunk off the field, and it wandered around the infield for an hour.

BINGHAMTON BINGOES

League: New York State League
City: Binghamton, NY
Years: 1885, 1892-1894, 1899-1919

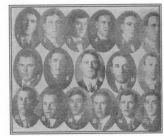

1909 Binghamton Bingoes
—National Baseball Hall of Fame Library. Cooperstown, NY

The Binghamton Bingoes team name has nothing to do with the famous game of luck. "Bingo," or "Bingo Town," is a nickname for the city of Binghamton. It isn't uncommon to hear someone in central New York these days say "I'm going to Bingo," before a ride to Binghamton. The game of Bingo came to the United States in 1929, decades after the Bingoes played in the New York State League. Today the Double-A Binghamton Mets keep the spirit of the Bingoes alive with a mascot named Bingo the Bee.

Not to Be Confused With: Bonham Bingers

Between the Lines: Baseball Hall of Famer Willie Keeler got his start with the Binghamton Bingoes. Keeler collected a hit and made an error in his first professional game for the Bingoes in 1892. He'd go on to win two batting titles and coin the famous phrase "hit 'em where they ain't."

New York

ILION TYPEWRITERS

League: New York State League
City: Ilion, NY
Years: 1901-1904

1904 Ilion Typewriters
—National Baseball Hall of Fame Library.
Cooperstown, NY

In a name that probably befriended sportswriters covering the team, the Ilion Typewriters printed through the New York State League for four years beginning in 1901. The Typewriters took their name after the Ilion-based Remington Typewriter Company, most known for producing the Remington Standard 2 Typewriter in 1878. This model was considered ahead of its time and was the prototype for future typewriters.

Not to Be Confused With: Panama City Papermakers

Between the Lines: The 1904 Typewriters finished 19 games over .500 because of two brothers. Bill Hinchman and Harry Hinchman excelled for Ilion in '04. Bill would lead the National League in triples 12 years later.

JAMESTOWN JAMMERS

League: New York-Penn League
City: Jamestown, NY
Years: 1994-Present

The Jamestown Jammers revamped their logo and mascot before the 2006 season, substituting their original ferocious Tasmanian devil logo to a loveable bunch-of-grapes motif. Along with the mascot Bubba Grape, the new look Jammers reflect the grape-growing history of the Jamestown area. The city of 35,000 is situated in the core of the Chautauqua County grape region.

Not to Be Confused With: Atlanta Wind Jammers

Between the Lines: Ten years before completing the most famous stolen base in Boston Red Sox history, Dave Roberts stole 12 bases for the Jamestown Jammers.

OSWEGO STARCHBOXES

League: International League
City: Oswego, NY
Years: 1886-1887

The slogan of Oswego, New York, is "where the water never ends," giving a charming description of its port location on Lake Ontario. In the formative years of Minor League Baseball, Oswego was the city where the team nicknames never ended, with many distinctive labels in rapid succession like the Oswego Sweegs, Oswego Starchboxes and Oswego Oswegos. The Starchboxes were named after the nearby Kingsford's Starch Factory.

Not to Be Confused With: New Haven Nutmegs

Between the Lines: Financial reports from this era show minor league teams in central New York with player payrolls of under $50 and spending less than $3 for a season's worth of washing uniforms.

Mike Mattimore played for the Oswego Starchboxes in 1886
—Library of Congress photo

POUGHKEEPSIE HONEY BUGS

League: New York-New Jersey League
City: Poughkeepsie, NY
Years: 1913-1914

1914 Poughkeepsie Honey Bugs
—National Baseball Hall of Fame Library.
Cooperstown, NY

The Poughkeepsie Honey Bugs doesn't sound like a very stern team name but it actually stood for hard work and energy. Poughkeepsie was developing in the early 1850s with entrepreneurs shaping the industry of the area. When Poughkeepsie officially became a city in 1854, a city seal was crafted with a beehive in the center of the logo to symbolize teamwork and effort. Poughkeepsie has used an assortment of bee references since, like the local Busy Bee restaurant and the Poughkeepsie Honey Bugs professional baseball team.

Not to Be Confused With: Lowell Honeys, Piedmont Drybugs

Between the Lines: A Danbury Hatters speedster named Culcahy astonished Honey Bugs fans by stealing second base, third base and home on successive pitches against Poughkeepsie on July 13, 1913.

SCHENECTADY FROG ALLEYS

League: New York State League
City: Schenectady, NY
Years: 1903

The Schenectady Frog Alleys hopped over all other teams in the Class B New York State League in 1903, finishing in first place. The city of Schenectady is set where the Hudson River and Mohawk River converge, leaving plenty of opportunities for reptiles and frog alleys.

Not to Be Confused With:
Portland Webfeet

Between the Lines: The first-place Frog Alleys pitching ace was Del Mason, whose 24-7 record was the best in the New York State League. One year later Mason stormed into the Major Leagues with the Washington Senators.

1903 Schenectady Frog Alleys
—National Baseball Hall of Fame Library. Cooperstown, NY

UTICA BREWMASTERS

League: New York State League
City: Utica, NY
Years: 2007

Donovan Stadium—former home of the Utica Brewmasters
—Courtesy of Brian Merzbach

The Utica Brewmasters team name acknowledges the beer history in eastern New York. Utica Club beer was the first type of beer sold in the United States legally after Prohibition Laws were overturned. The Brewmasters played at Murnane Field's Donovan Stadium against New York State League squads like the Rome Coppers, Oneida Barge Bucs and Herkimer Trailbusters. The Brewmasters first game was over 120 years after Utica's first team, the Utica Pentups, who took the field in 1885 in the original New York State League.

Not to Be Confused With: Peoria Distillers, Helena Brewers, Clarksdale Ginners

Between the Lines: The Brewmasters hired Utica native and three-time Major League All-Star Dave Cash to manage the club. Cash was ejected from the first game in team history for arguing balls and strikes.

YONKERS HOOT OWLS

League: Northeast League
City: Yonkers, NY
Years: 1995

A team just outside New York City called the Hoot Owls may bring the honking of car horns to mind for the reason behind the team name, but a hoot owl is an actual species of owl. Generally found near a pond or lake, hoot owls are sometimes referred to as rain owls or striped owls. Playing in the Independent Northeast League, the Hoot Owls won just 12 games in 64 tries in 1995, finishing behind teams like the Newburgh Nighthawks and Mohawk Valley Landsharks.

Not to Be Confused With: Brandon Grey Owls, Rutherford County Owls, Bend Timber Hawks, Hattiesburg Woodpeckers

Between the Lines: The Hoot Owls manager was eight-time Gold Glove winner Paul Blair, who was known for his acrobatic catches throughout his Major League career with the Orioles, Yankees and Reds.

ASHEVILLE TOURISTS

League: South Atlantic League
City: Asheville, NC
Years: 1914, 1925, 1976-Present

The Asheville Tourists have the funniest scoreboard in Minor League Baseball. The top line reads "Visitors" and the bottom line says "Tourists." Tourism in Asheville is a huge business. The city is nestled in the Great Smoky and Blue Ridge Mountain ranges. The nearby Great Smoky Mountains National Park is the most visited National Park in the United States.

Not to Be Confused With: Norwich Navigators

Between the Lines: Hall of Famer Cal Ripken Jr., University of North Carolina Basketball Coach Roy Williams and San Diego Padres outfielder Cameron Maybin all have something in common—they were Asheville Tourists bat boys!

CAROLINA MUDCATS

League: Southern League
City: Zebulon, NC
Years: 1991-Present

The Carolina Mudcats team name originated in a river nowhere near their stadium. Before relocating to North Carolina, the Columbus Mudcats played in Columbus, Georgia. Golden Park in Columbus is a foul ball away from the Chattahoochee River, so Mudcats, a synonym for a catfish, was an appropriate name. The logo and team name were so popular that when the Mudcats moved cities, they brought the team name with them.

Not to Be Confused With: Altoona Mud Turtles

Between the Lines: The 2003 Mudcats are considered one of the best Double-A teams in history. Carolina won the Southern League that year and featured future Major League All-Stars Miguel Cabrera, Adrian Gonzalez and Dontrelle Willis.

GREENSBORO GRASSHOPPERS

League: South Atlantic League
City: Greensboro, NC
Years: 2005-Present

When Greensboro's Minor League Baseball team built a new stadium and changed major league affiliates in 2005, they also changed team nicknames from Bats to Grasshoppers. Their inaugural season as the Greensboro Grasshoppers was marked with multiple hopping promotions, like the release of live grasshoppers throughout the stadium on opening night. With the Grasshoppers trying to jump over the Lexington Legends and the rest of the South Atlantic League, the team borrowed an actual Grasshopper Cannon from a local historical society. The cannon, created by the British in the 1700s, is a target of fans walking in to First Horizon Park, where they rub the cannon for good luck.

Not to Be Confused With: Spokane Bunchgrassers, Hattiesburg Pinetoppers

Between the Lines: A Midland Cubs game in 1972 was postponed because of a grasshopper plague.

KANNAPOLIS INTIMIDATORS

League: South Atlantic League
City: Kannapolis, NC
Years: 2001-Present

The Kannapolis Intimidators team name was modeled after their owner's nickname. In November of 2000, NASCAR legend Dale Earnhardt was part of the group that purchased the Single-A Piedmont Boll Weevils and moved the team to his hometown of Kannapolis. Earnhardt was known as "The Intimidator." These days, the Intimidators try to scare teams like the Augusta GreenJackets and Asheville Tourists in the Single-A South Atlantic League.

Not to Be Confused With: East Chicago Conquistadors

Between the Lines: The Intimidators outlasted the Charleston RiverDogs 4-3 in a 21-inning playoff marathon on September 7, 2005. Just over 300 fans remained when the game ended in the early morning of September 8.

RALEIGH-DURHAM TRIANGLES

League: Carolina League
City: Durham, NC
Years: 1970-1971

The Raleigh-Durham Triangles squared off on baseball diamonds in the Single-A Carolina League starting in 1970. The Triangles team name was a reference to the triangle region of North Carolina, which includes Raleigh, Durham and Chapel Hill. The area was originally called "The Research Triangle," because of the research being done at Duke University, North Carolina State University and the University of North Carolina.

Not to Be Confused With: Waterloo Diamonds

Between the Lines: Nardi Contreras pitched for the Triangles as a 19-year-old. Contreras has gone on to become a Major League pitching coach and now oversees the minor league development of pitchers for the New York Yankees.

THOMASVILLE CHAIR MAKERS

League: North Carolina State League
City: Thomasville, NC
Years: 1937

The Thomasville Chair Makers probably had the most comfortable dugout in the Class D North Carolina State League. Thomasville is known for furniture manufacturing and is referred to as "Chair Town" and "Chair City." In downtown Thomasville there is a 30-foot-tall replica of a Duncan Phyfe armchair, believed to be the tallest chair in the world. The Chair Makers rocked when playing against teams like the Cooleemee Weavers and Mooresville Moors.

Finch Field—former home of the Thomasville Chair Makers —Courtesy of Brian Merzbach

Not to Be Confused With: High Point Furniture Makers

Between the Lines: The second-place Chair Makers had five players selected to the North Carolina State League All-Star team in 1937. Walter Sessi was not one of them, yet it was Sessi who went on to play in the Major Leagues, winning a World Series with the Cardinals in 1946.

GRAND FORKS FLICKER TAILS

League: Central International League
City: Grand Forks, ND
Years: 1912-1915

Flicker tails were a popular creature in North Dakota by 1913, as the University of North Dakota's athletic teams used the same moniker at that time. The lightly colored ground squirrels still roam the northern plains. The folks in Grand Forks got more creative with their baseball team nicknames as time went on. Before the Flicker Tails, the Class D Northern League team in the area was unoriginally called the Grand Forks Forkers.

Not to Be Confused With: Abilene Prairie Dogs, Albany Polecats

Between the Lines: Carter Wilson filled Flicker Tails fans with pride on May 23, 1913 when he threw a no-hitter against the Virginia Ore Diggers.

John Peters played for the Grand Forks Flicker Tails in 1914 —Library of Congress photo

GRAND FORKS VARMINTS

League: Prairie League
City: Grand Forks, ND
Years: 1996-1997

The Grand Forks Varmints were named after the agricultural side of North Dakota's third-largest city. A varmint refers to a larger animal, like a coyote, invading farms and vandalizing crops.

Kraft Field—former home of the Grand Forks Varmints
—Courtesy of University of North Dakota

Some may mention varmints when talking guns; varmint rifles are used by farm owners to shoot animals interfering with their land. During their two years of existence, the Grand Forks Varmints were one of four teams in North Dakota playing in the Prairie League, but also tried to raid out of state opponents like the Southern Minny Stars and Green Bay Sultans.

Not to Be Confused With: Dothan Boll Weevils

Between the Lines: Varmints manager Mike Verdi came from a baseball pedigree. His father Frank Verdi was a longtime manager in professional baseball and famously entered one Major League game without having a chance to bat.

MINOT WHY NOTS

League: Northern League
City: Minot, ND
Years: 1917

Minot (pronounced MY-not) North Dakota is the city most often joked about in the Air Force. When discussing base assignments, personnel suggest "Why Not Minot?" This leads to the punch line "freezin's the reason." The rhyming question "Why Not Minot?" is to this day the unofficial slogan in the city of 36,000. The Why Nots may have asked why the Fargo-Moorhead Graingrowers beat them by 12 games in the standings that year, but the Warren Wanderers were the ones asking questions after they finished fourth in the Class D Northern League in 1917, the only team behind Minot in the standings.

Not to Be Confused With:
Amsterdam-Johnstown-Gloversville Hyphens

Between the Lines: After the Northern League disbanded during the Why Nots only season, manager George Brautigan focused on making a comeback as a player. Four years later he succeeded, hitting .305 for the Winnipeg Maroons.

Ohio

LAKE ERIE CRUSHERS

League: Frontier League
City: Avon, OH
Years: 2009-Present

The Lake Erie Crushers play in Avon, Ohio, and use a regional name to welcome fans from the cities and towns surrounding Avon. The team name goes beyond the visual of a player crushing a baseball. It ties in two local occupations, the crushing of grapes by local wineries and the crushing of steel by the local construction industry. The Crushers lineup hopes to step on the pitching staffs of Frontier League teams like the Gateway Grizzlies and Kalamazoo Kings.

Not to Be Confused With: St. Catharines Stompers

Between the Lines: The Crushers had a suspenseful championship run in 2009, winning the best of five championship series against the River City Rascals after losing the first two games.

SANDUSKY SUDS

League: Ohio State League
City: Sandusky, OH
Years: 1887

The Sandusky Suds team name makes you wonder if the team always had clean uniforms. Sandusky, Ohio, is set on Lake Erie and is known for fishing and boating in the Sandusky Bay. Sandusky's professional baseball teams over the years have often used boating-related names like the Suds, the Sandusky Fish Eaters and the Sandusky Sailors.

Not to Be Confused With: Norfolk Tides

Between the Lines: It wasn't always easy getting fans to the ballpark in the 1880s. On May 27, 1885, the Allentown vs. Lancaster game was cancelled when only one fan showed up. Everyone else was at a popular parade nearby.

TOLEDO MUD HENS

League: International League
City: Toledo, OH
Years: 1897-1914, 1919-1955, 1965-Present

Scot Drucker—Toledo Mud Hens
—Courtesy of Paul Nelson

The Toledo Mud Hens team name is as popular and celebrated as any in the history of Minor League Baseball. The Mud Hens name was first attached to Toledo's baseball team in 1896 and has been continuously used since 1965. The Mud Hens team name became nationally known through the television series *M*A*S*H*, featuring character Max Klinger, an outspoken Mud Hens fan on the show. Klinger was played by actor and Toledo native Jamie Farr. When the Mud Hens began play back before the turn of the 20th century, their home was Bay View Park, an area surrounded by marshlands occupied by long-legged birds called mud hens.

Not to Be Confused With: Merrillville Muddogs

Between the Lines: In 1982 Toledo Mud Hens infielder Randy Bush hit a home run that traveled 200 miles. His long ball went over the right field fence in Charleston, West Virginia, and landed on a moving train. The coal train didn't stop until hours later.

YOUNGSTOWN PUDDLERS

League: Interstate League
City: Youngstown, OH
Years: 1896-1898

Hall of Famer Elmer Flick played for the Youngstown Puddlers in 1896
—Library of Congress photo

Before you picture a team that played in a stadium without a tarp, we should point out the Youngstown Puddlers team name actually had nothing to do with water or puddles. In Youngstown, Ohio, in the late 1800s a puddler was an industrial worker specializing in molten metal. The Puddlers first played in the Interstate League in 1896. Other teams in the Interstate League during this time also used blue-collar worker-styled names, like the Saginaw Lumbermen, Wheeling Nailers and Fort Wayne Farmers.

Not to Be Confused With:
Hot Springs Vaporites

Between the Lines: Before winning batting titles in the Major Leagues, Elmer Flick started his career with the Youngstown Puddlers. Flick was such a great offensive player in the early 1900s that Cleveland management turned down a trade proposal that would have brought them Ty Cobb in return. Flick was elected to the National Baseball Hall of Fame in 1963.

Ohio

Oklahoma

ZANESVILLE FLOOD SUFFERERS

League: Interstate League
City: Zanesville, OH
Years: 1913

In an effort to rebuild morale after a devastating flood in 1913, Zanesville's local Minor League Baseball team was named the Flood Sufferers. The flood in 1913 ruined parts of southern Ohio and the small towns along the Muskingum River. The Flood Sufferers baseball team dried up during the 1913 Class B Interstate League season, finishing last behind the Youngstown Steelmen and Steubenville Stubs.

Not to Be Confused With: Boise Irrigators

Sad Sam Jones played for the 1913 Zanesville Flood Sufferers
—Library of Congress photo

Between the Lines: Sad Sam Jones signed with the Flood Sufferers as a 20-year-old in 1913. Later during his 22-year Major League career, sportswriters dubbed him "Sad Sam" because he wore his cap low so nobody could see his face.

LAWTON MEDICINE MEN

League: Texas-Oklahoma League
City: Lawton, OK
Years: 1911

Lawton, Oklahoma, is set right on Medicine Creek and Medicine Park, and that location is the source of this unique team nickname. The Medicine Men had a prescription for losing in 1911, finishing in last place behind the Durant Educators, Gainesville Blue Ribbons and the rest of the Class D Texas-Oklahoma League.

Not to Be Confused With: Medicine Hat Hatters

Between the Lines: The Texas-Oklahoma League playoffs ended in controversy in 1911 when the Wichita Falls Irish Lads refused to play against the Cleburne Railroaders after a dispute over which club received the ticket revenue. The Railroaders were declared champions.

 *Pennsylvania*

PENDLETON BUCKAROOS

League: Western Tri-State League
City: Pendleton, OR
Years: 1912-1914

A Pendleton Buckaroos baseball game was the second-most popular summertime activity in Pendleton, Oregon, in the early 1900s. The team was named after the Pendleton Roundup. The rodeo is held each September and is one of the ten largest in the world. The Pendleton Buckaroos bulled through the Class D Western Tri-State League against the Baker City Golddiggers and Walla Walla Bears.

1914 Pendleton Buckaroos
—National Baseball Hall of Fame Library.
Cooperstown, NY

Not to Be Confused With: Boise Buckskins

Between the Lines: With a name like Homer Harold Haworth, you'd think he was a power hitter. Not so. The 1913 Buckaroos catcher hit seven home runs in over 1,100 career at bats.

ALTOONA CURVE

League: Eastern League
City: Altoona, PA
Years: 1999-Present

The Altoona Curve threw a curveball with this team name. In addition to the baseball meaning, the name Curve also involves something traveling faster than a breaking pitch. Horseshoe Curve is a section of railroad near Altoona constructed as a means for trains to get through the Allegheny Mountains. Horseshoe Curve is still considered an engineering masterpiece, making it an appropriate tribute to this region's history.

Not to Be Confused With: South Bend Benders

Between the Lines: The Curve snag laughs once a year during their "Awful Night" promotion, where they post "failure averages" instead of batting averages on the scoreboard, display players' baby photos on the video board and crack jokes on the public address microphone as hitters walk to the plate.

ERIE SEAWOLVES

League: Eastern League
City: Erie, PA
Years: 1995-Present

Although the team plays just miles from the Pennsylvania shores of Lake Erie, the SeaWolves team nickname does not refer to an aquatic creature of any kind. A Seawolf is slang term for a Pirate, and when the franchise moved to Erie in 1995, they wanted to have a team nickname similar to their major league affiliate, the Pittsburgh Pirates. These days, the SeaWolves are trying to sail through the likes of the New Britain Rock Cats and Connecticut Defenders.

Not to Be Confused With: Portland Sea Dogs, Cedartown Sea Cows, Helena Seaporters

Between the Lines: It was an easy decision for the Detroit Tigers to call up Justin Verlander from the SeaWolves in 2005. Verlander made three starts for Erie and had an ERA of 0.00.

LEHIGH VALLEY IRONPIGS

League: International League
City: Allentown, PA
Years: 2008-Present

The latest entry into the Triple-A International League has one of the league's most unique team names, while also tying into the Allentown, Pennsylvania, identity. The IronPigs moniker touches on one of the leading occupations in Allentown: steel production. Pig iron is a carbon-based form of iron used in the production of steel. The *Morning Call*, Allentown's daily paper, along with the Lehigh Valley team staff, operated a name the team contest. After slicing through 3,500 entries, the contest was narrowed to Crushers, Gobblers, IronPigs, Keystones, Phantastics, Phillies, Vulcans and Woodchucks, with IronPigs beating the other seven candidates.

Not to Be Confused With: Toledo Iron Men

Between the Lines: The IronPigs have the most creative grounds crew in baseball. The "Dancing Dirt Dudes" captivate fans in Lehigh Valley with rehearsed acts set to music while they drag the infield between innings.

SHAMOKIN SHAMMIES

League: New York-Pennsylvania League
City: Shamokin, PA
Years: 1925

These days, you may know a shammy as a suede leather cloth for cleaning automobiles but the Shamokin Shammies professional baseball team took its name after the city name. Shamokin, Pennsylvania, is sometimes referred to as "Shammy." The Shammies finished last in the Class C New York-Pennsylvania League in 1925 behind the Scranton Miners, Binghamton Triplets and York White Roses.

Not to Be Confused With: San Angelo Sheep Herders, New Jersey Jackals

Between the Lines: The Shammies signed Amos "Lightning" Strunk to draw more fans in 1925. Strunk was a legend in the region after winning three World Series for Connie Mack's Philadelphia Athletics from 1910-1914.

Amos Strunk played for the Shamokin Shammies in 1925
—Library of Congress photo

SLIPPERY ROCK SLIDERS

League: Frontier League
City: Slippery Rock, PA
Years: 2007

Jack Critchfield Park—former home of the Slippery Rock Sliders
—Courtesy of Brian Merzbach

You could call the professional baseball team in Slippery Rock, Pennsylvania, just about anything and it would be included on the list of unique team names. The Slippery Rock Sliders were able to create a team name tying into the city name, while also doubling as the name of a pitch in baseball. A name the team contest before the inaugural season brought in 92 submissions, and Sliders received more votes than the proposed Boulders, Rockers or Sluggers.

Not to Be Confused With: Rock Island Rocks, Williamsport Crosscutters

Between the Lines: Sliders manager Greg Jelks knows the taste of big league glory. He played 10 seasons in the minors, but did reach the Major Leagues, going 1-for-10 with a double for the 1987 Phillies.

Rhode Island

South Carolina

WOONSOCKET TROTTERS

League: Atlantic Association
City: Woonsocket, RI
Years: 1908

You may think the Woonsocket Trotters name was a reference to a home run trot, but this team name actually got inspiration from a local champion horse. The owners of a champion trotter horse named Ruth Dillon lived in Woonsocket and in 1908 the horse was the athletic star of the town. Six seasons later the newly named Woonsocket Speeders finished behind the first place Fall River Spindles in the Class C Colonial League.

Not to Be Confused With: Dakota Rattlers

Between the Lines: The Trotters manager was John Leighton, who played in the Major Leagues in 1890 for the Syracuse Stars.

ANDERSON JOES

League: South Coast League
City: Anderson, SC
Years: 2007

Anderson Memorial Stadium—former home of the Anderson Joes
—Courtesy of Brian Merzbach

Believe it or not, there was a professional baseball team named after a legendary player banned from baseball. In the early 1900s, Joe Jackson played a minor league game in Anderson, South Carolina. While it looked like an average game in the next day's box score, this was the game where Jackson played in his stockings because his cleats gave him blisters, creating the nickname "Shoeless Joe Jackson." The Anderson Joes took the field in the South Coast League in 2007, named after this footnote in baseball history.

Not to Be Confused With: Johnstown Johnnies

Between the Lines: The Joes manager ended up playing for a rival team. When the Joes started poorly, manager Desi Wilson added himself to the playing roster and Kash Beauchamp became the new manager. Wilson was traded to the South Georgia Peanuts weeks later.

CHARLESTON RAINBOWS

League: South Atlantic League
City: Charleston, SC
Years: 1985-1993

There was no pot of gold at the end of a Charleston Rainbows season. In a nine-year stretch using the colorful team name, the Rainbows finished above .500 just twice. The Rainbows played a few miles from Rainbow Row in Charleston, a famous line of vibrant mid-1700s style homes.

Not to Be Confused With: Wellsville Rainmakers, Auburn Sunsets

Between the Lines: Roberto Alomar, Sandy Alomar, Carlos Baerga and Kevin Seitzer all played Single-A ball for the Rainbows.

GREENVILLE DRIVE

League: South Atlantic League
City: Greenville, SC
Years: 2006-Present

The Greenville Drive was one of the few nicknames we found that is also a verb. The Drive team name was selected after the *Greenville News* held a name the team contest, bringing over 500 submissions to the local newspaper. Other suggestions included the Barefooters, Yard Dogs, Crescents, Downtowners, Fire Ants, Goons, Grits, Motors and Uptowners. Greenville has an automotive connection, making the team name Drive applicable. The Michelin Tire North American headquarters are located in Greenville.

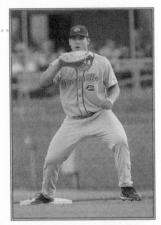

Anthony Rizzo—Greenville Drive
—Courtesy of Billy Crowe

Not to Be Confused With: Flint Vehicles

Between the Lines: Benches emptied during a Drive playoff game against the Lakewood BlueClaws in September 2010 after a collision between Greenville's Derrik Gibson and Lakewood catcher Sebastian Valle. Four players were ejected after the brawl.

South Dakota

HURON HEATERS

League: North Central League
City: Huron, SD
Years: 1994

With an average January temperature below 10 degrees in Huron, some form of heating is necessary for all residents. Mindful of this necessity, and factoring in the dual meaning of a heater as a synonym for a fastball, the Huron Heaters team name was selected in 1994 for the newest team in the North Central League. Traveling north to play the Regina Cyclones, or east to take on the Minneapolis Loons, the Heaters finished last in their only season of existence.

Not to Be Confused With: St. Paul Freezers

Between the Lines: There was a World Series ring floating around the Heaters clubhouse. Manager Glenn Gulliver played for the 1983 champion Baltimore Orioles.

MITCHELL KERNELS

League: South Dakota League
City: Mitchell, SD
Years: 1920-1923, 1936-1937, 1939-1940

The Mitchell Kernels played in the city most likely to have a team named after corn. Mitchell, South Dakota, is home to "The World's Only Corn Palace," and holds an annual Corn Palace Festival. Away from the cornfield, and on the ball field, the Kernels had a stalk of championships, winning three in a row from 1920-1922 against teams like the Jamestown Jimkotans.

1922 Mitchell Kernels
—National Baseball Hall of Fame Library. Cooperstown, NY

Not to Be Confused With: Akron Acorns

Between the Lines: Del Paddock played in the Major Leagues with the Chicago White Sox and New York Yankees as an infielder and a decade later tried to refine his skills as a pitcher for the 1920 Kernels. He never returned to the big leagues as a hurler.

SIOUX FALLS CANARIES

League: American Association
City: Sioux Falls, SD
Years: 1902-1903, 1921, 1924, 1933-1942, 1946-1953, 1993-Present

When coming across the Sioux Falls Canaries team name, you may ask if there are really canaries in South Dakota. The answer is no, but the professional baseball team in South Dakota's largest city still carries the nickname. The story behind the name dates back to 1902, when the Class D Iowa-South Dakota League team in Sioux Falls named their team the Canaries. The team wore yellow jerseys in honor of the popular comic strip character "Yellowman," and players remarked how they looked like canaries on the field.

Not to Be Confused With: Missoula Osprey

Between the Lines: The Canaries played in the earliest morning game in professional baseball history on May 8, 2005. The St. Paul Saints scheduled the 5:35 a.m. game as a Mother's Day promotion. The Canaries had to wake up at 4:00 a.m. to go to Midway Stadium in St. Paul and warm up.

CHATTANOOGA LOOKOUTS

League: Southern League
City: Chattanooga, TN
Years: 1885-1886, 1901-1902, 1909-1961, 1963-1965, 1976-Present

Chattanooga is set near Lookout Mountain, where Tennessee, Georgia and Alabama meet. The rolling green hills can be seen beyond the outfielders at AT&T Field in Chattanooga. The Lookouts now combat teams like the Jacksonville Suns and Tennessee Smokies just a few miles away from the site of a more historical matchup, the First Battle of Chattanooga—a Civil War battle held at Lookout Mountain in 1862.

Luis Bolivar—Chattanooga Lookouts
—Meeks and Norris Photography

Not to Be Confused With: Fayetteville Generals

Between the Lines: Female pitcher Jackie Mitchell struck out Babe Ruth and Lou Gehrig during an exhibition game between the Lookouts and New York Yankees. When the Lookouts signed Mitchell in 1931, she became just the second woman to play professional baseball.

COLUMBIA MULES

League: Alabama-Tennessee League
City: Columbia, TN
Years: 1921, 1996-1997

Red Smith managed the 1921 Columbia Mules
—Library of Congress photo

If you asked someone in Columbia, Tennessee, why their professional baseball team was called the Mules, they would definitely know the answer. Columbia is known for its association with Mules, hosting "Mule Day" each April. The festivities include the annual Mule Day Parade, and the crowning of that year's "Mule Queen." When Columbia brought baseball back in the mid-1990s, they brought the Mules back as well, naming their team in the Big South League the Columbia Mules, forming an immediate in-state rivalry with the Tennessee Tomahawks.

Not to Be Confused With: Greeneville Burley Cubs

Between the Lines: Playoff fever swept through the city when the Mules beat the Tomahawks in the first round of the post-season in 1996. Their championship aspirations were halted when the Greenville Bluesmen swept the Mules in the next round.

NASHVILLE SOUNDS

League: Pacific Coast League
City: Nashville, TN
Years: 1978-Present

Nashville is the center of the country music industry and the home of the Country Music Hall of Fame and Museum. When professional baseball returned to Nashville in 1978, owner Larry Schmittou selected the name Sounds to honor the city's place in the world of music. Schmittou even brought on country music artists Larry Gatlin, Jerry Reed and Conway Twitty to become Sounds' stockholders.

Not to Be Confused With: Piqua Picks

Between the Lines: Retiring uniform numbers in the minor leagues is uncommon, but the Sounds have two retired jerseys. Numbers 00 (Skeeter Barnes) and 18 (Don Mattingly) will never be worn by a Sound again.

SPRINGFIELD BLANKET MAKERS

League: Kitty League
City: Springfield, TN
Years: 1923

The Springfield Blanket Makers ended their first season on the wrong side of the bed, finishing last in the Class D Kitty League. The Blanket Makers selected their name because of the Springfield Woolen Mills, a major blanket manufacturer in Springfield, Tennessee. Much of the company's business came from producing blankets for military members overseas.

Not to Be Confused With: Lowell Spinners

Between the Lines: The man in charge of the Kitty League was a true multitasker. Dr. Frank Bassett served as League President, Treasurer and Secretary.

BEAUMONT GOLDEN GATORS

League: Texas League
City: Beaumont, TX
Years: 1983-1986

Vincent-Beck Stadium—former home of the Beaumont Golden Gators
—Courtesy of Brian Merzbach

The Beaumont Golden Gators team name was partially borrowed from its previous residence. After the 1982 season, the Amarillo Gold Sox moved from northern Texas to the Texas coast. The team kept the gold adjective in the moniker, but added a swampy twist, becoming the Beaumont Golden Gators. Beaumont is set right along the Gulf of Mexico, so a reference to an alligator in the team name became appropriate. Also, Beaumont is geographically a point of the Golden Triangle portion of Texas, along with nearby cities Orange and Port Arthur.

Not to Be Confused With: Goldsboro Goldbugs

Between the Lines: Long before he was fined for tweeting after an ejection, Ozzie Guillen played for the Golden Gators in Double-A as a 19-year-old in 1983.

HOUSTON WANDERERS

League: South Texas League
City: Houston, TX
Years: 1904

1904 Houston Wanderers
—National Baseball Hall of Fame Library.
Cooperstown, NY

Some teams throughout the history of Minor League Baseball have used traveling-related names to describe the frequent movement of a team during a season, but the Houston Wanderers team name described the growth of Houston in the early 1900s. When oil was discovered in the Beaumont and Houston area, the potential for wealth brought thousands to Texas. Houston's population doubled from 1900 to 1910 because of new residents wandering in from elsewhere.

Not to Be Confused With: Arkansas Travelers, Lancaster Barnstormers

Between the Lines: The early days of Minor League Baseball in Texas were truly the Wild West. In the late 1800s a game in Austin ended early when a wild bull charged at an Austin outfielder.

LUBBOCK CRICKETS

League: Texas-Louisiana League
City: Lubbock, TX
Years: 1995-1998

Born and raised in Lubbock, Texas, Buddy Holly's band "The Crickets" was the inspiration for this team nickname. Two years after their 1995 Texas-Louisiana League Championship, the only chirps heard in Lubbock were from actual crickets. The team disbanded after drawing just 800 fans per game.

Not to Be Confused With: Pocomoke City Salamanders

Dan Law Field—former home of the Lubbock Crickets
—Courtesy of Texas Tech University

Between the Lines: Lubbock won the title in 1995 in part because of the wisdom of Frank DiPino, the lefty who continued his career with the Crickets after pitching 12 seasons in the Major Leagues.

MIDLAND ROCKHOUNDS

League: Texas League
City: Midland, TX
Years: 1999-Present

While the Midland RockHounds are currently barking their way through the Double-A Texas League against the Corpus Christi Hooks and Frisco RoughRiders, the nickname RockHounds actually has nothing to do with a dog. A rock hound is a term used for geologists searching for valuable stones, and in the Permian Basin section of Texas, quests for minerals are common.

Not to Be Confused With: Huntington Jewels

Between the Lines: Former RockHound Mark Kiger became the first player in over 120 years to make his Major League debut in the playoffs. He suited up for the Oakland A's against Detroit in the 2006 ALCS after spending the first half of the 2006 season with Midland.

ROUND ROCK EXPRESS

League: Pacific Coast League
City: Round Rock, TX
Years: 2000-Present

When Dallas area sportswriters nicknamed pitcher Nolan Ryan "The Ryan Express," little did they know the nickname would transfer to a Minor League Baseball team years later. The all-time strikeout leader now is part of an ownership group for two minor league teams as part of his post-retirement business life, and the team under his control in Round Rock, Texas, was named the Express when the team moved to the Austin suburb in 2000.

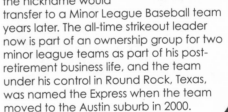

Not to Be Confused With: Council Bluffs Rails

Between the Lines: The Express used the most comedic pitcher in baseball in 2010. Will Ferrell wore a Round Rock uniform and played the role of fictitious pitcher Rojo Johnson during a between-innings skit.

SWEETWATER SWATTERS

League: West Texas League
City: Sweetwater, TX
Years: 1920-1922, 1949-1951

Sweetwater, Texas, is world renown as home of "The World's Largest Rattlesnake Roundup." But don't infer swatter is some sort of rattlesnake capturing term, because the annual event began in 1958, nearly 40 years after the Swatters began swiping the Clovis Buzzers, Eastland Judges and the rest of the Class D West Texas League. The nickname was a compliment to Sweetwater's hitting ability. The Swatters finished first in the West Texas League in 1921, just a game and a half ahead of the Abilene Eagles.

Pop-Boy Smith managed the 1921 Sweetwater Swatters
—Library of Congress photo

Not to Be Confused With: Lodi Crushers, Muscatine Wallopers

Between the Lines: Swatters manager John Bottarini had a good reason for not playing more than 26 Major League games. His Chicago Cubs teammate Gabby Hartnett was also a catcher—and is now in the Hall of Fame.

TEXARKANA CASKETMAKERS

League: Texas League
City: Texarkana, TX
Years: 1902

On both sides of State Line Avenue in Texarkana, Texas, and Texarkana, Arkansas, wood manufacturing is a major source of employment. This industry has led to the assembly of many wooden products over the years, including caskets. Sadly, the Texarkana Casketmakers had to make their own casket in 1902, when the team disbanded, failing to compete with the Corsicana Oil Citys or Paris Parisites in the Class D Texas League. These days, the Texarkana Gunslingers play the Bay Area Toros, McKinney Blue Thunder and the rest of the Continental Baseball League.

Not to Be Confused With: Petersburg Trunkmakers

Between the Lines: The Casketmakers had to move their game from Corsicana to Ennis, Texas, on June 15, 1902 because playing ball on Sundays was banned in Corsicana.

TYLER WILDCATTERS

League: Texas-Louisiana League
City: Tyler, TX
Years: 1994-1997

A wildcatter is defined as "a person engaged in speculative well drilling in areas known to be unproductive." Tyler's team in the Texas-Louisiana League lived up to the unproductive definition, never qualifying for the playoffs in its four-year existence from 1994-1997. They were beaten by teams like the Corpus Christi Barracudas, Beaumont Bullfrogs and Pueblo Bighorns.

Mike Carter Field—former home of the Tyler Wildcatters —Courtesy of Brian Merzbach

Not to Be Confused With: Tulsa Drillers, Beaumont Oil Gushers

Between the Lines: Larry Carter threw the only no-hitter in Wildcatters history on June 21, 1994. He was also the team's pitching coach.

WICHITA FALLS SPUDDERS

League: Texas League
City: Wichita Falls, TX
Years: 1920-1932, 1941-1942, 1947-1957

In the case of this nickname, a Spudder has nothing to do with a potato or a struggling automobile. The Wichita Falls Spudders name referred to a large, now outdated, piece of drilling equipment. Sometimes up to 40 feet long, a spudder was a long bar pushed into the ground to gather oil. Drilling in the Class B Texas League, the Spudders finished

1930 Wichita Falls Spudders
—National Baseball Hall of Fame Library. Cooperstown, NY

ahead of the Shreveport Gassers and Beaumont Explorers in 1920, and squashed the Galveston Sand Crabs two years later.

Not to Be Confused With: Odessa Oilers

Between the Lines: The Spudders game against the Fort Worth Panthers on August 30, 1922, was the first Texas League game broadcasted on the radio. The staff at WBAP radio gave recreated play by play from a downtown studio while receiving updates from a stringer at the ballpark.

OGDEN GUNNERS

League: Utah-Idaho League
City: Ogden, UT
Years: 1926-1928

The Ogden Gunners took their name after the gun production in Utah. Browning North America, a leading company in producing rifles and outdoor apparel, is headquartered a short drive from Ogden. The Gunners played in the Class C Utah-Idaho League, with opponents like the Twin Falls Bruins, Logan Collegians and Salt Lake City Bees. Ogden, just north of Salt Lake City, now hosts the Ogden Raptors of the Pioneer League. Their name reflects the dinosaur fossils once found in the area.

Not to Be Confused With: Greenville Buckshots, Salina Insurgents

Between the Lines: Hall of Famer Ernie Lombardi joined the Gunners in 1927 before winning two National League batting titles and playing in seven Major League All-Star Games.

ST. GEORGE ROADRUNNERS

League: Golden Baseball League
City: St. George, UT
Years: 2007-2010

While most people see the name roadrunner and think of the cartoon character, the long legged birds are quite common in southern Utah. The St. George RoadRunners opened their inaugural season in 2007, rapidly running into the Golden Baseball League against the San Diego Surf Dawgs, Chico Outlaws and Yuma Scorpions. As for the origination of the RoadRunners team name, baseball fans in Utah have a young fan to thank. Fifth grader Adam Kemp won an essay contest organized to name the team, and, as his reward, threw out the first pitch on opening day.

Not to Be Confused With: Headland Dixie Runners, North Wilkesboro Flashers

Between the Lines: The RoadRunners competed at Bruce Hurst Field, named for the St. George native who played 15 seasons in the Major Leagues.

SALT LAKE CITY ELDERS

League: Pacific National League
City: Salt Lake City, UT
Years: 1903-1904

It sounds like it might have been tough to find any rookies on the Salt Lake City Elders roster. The Elders team name actually wasn't a reflection of the ages of their players but a religious reference. An Elder is a title for members of the Melchizedek Priesthood in the Church of Jesus Christ of Latter-day Saints. Six seasons after the Elders finished 29 games behind the first-place Butte Miners in 1903, the Salt Lake City Mormons came knocking on the league's door, ready to follow in their elders' footsteps as the city's new team.

Not to Be Confused With: Parsons Preachers, St. Paul Apostles

Between the Lines: Salt Lake City outfielder Bobby Cherry accidentally trapped his arm in a hole on the outfield fence while chasing a fly ball in 1951. He was stuck in the fence, with the baseball resting right next to him while the batter rounded the bases.

MONTPELIER GOLDFISH

League: Quebec-Ontario-Vermont League
City: Montpelier, VT
Years: 1924

Joe Evers played for the Montpelier Goldfish in 1924
—Library of Congress photo

In their only year in the Class B Quebec-Ontario-Vermont League, the Montpelier Goldfish came up floating in last place. For a small state, Vermont has produced its share of unique minor league nicknames. The Bellows Falls Sulphites and Brattleboro Islanders played in the 1911 Class D Twin States League. The Springfield-Charlestown Hyphens were in that league too, taking their team name after the dash connecting the neighboring towns of Springfield, Vermont, and Charlestown, New Hampshire.

Not to Be Confused With: Centralia Pets

Between the Lines: Former Goldfish player Joe Evers ended up with the same resume as Moonlight Graham, the player made famous in the movie *Field of Dreams*. Both Evers and Graham played in one Major League game, without getting a chance to bat.

VERMONT LAKE MONSTERS

League: New York-Penn League
City: Burlington, VT
Years: 2006-Present

For people in Vermont, the Vermont Lake Monsters nickname needs no explanation. Stories of an underwater creature in Lake Champlain have been passed on from generation to generation, with hundreds of reported sightings over the years. Some have called the creature "America's Loch Ness." Before changing team names in 2006, the franchise was called the Vermont Expos for 12 years. Vermont's team in the Single-A New York-Penn League was actually the last team in professional baseball to use the name Expos. The Montreal Expos moved to Washington, D.C., after the 2004 season, while the Vermont Expos lived on through 2005.

Not to Be Confused With: Lake County Captains, Great Lakes Loons

Between the Lines: The Lake Monsters ballpark opened before Fenway Park or Wrigley Field. Centennial Field was built in 1904 and has seen immortals like Tris Speaker and Ken Griffey Jr. play there.

BRISTOL STATE LINERS

League: Appalachian League
City: Bristol, VA
Years: 1921-1925

It is usually no challenge to pinpoint basic information like which state a Minor League Baseball team played in. For the 1921 Bristol State Liners, placing their location wasn't so easy. Bristol, Virginia, and Bristol, Tennessee, are governed as separate cities, but Bristol is considered a "twin city" with one side of town in Virginia, and the other in Tennessee. State Street in Bristol serves as the state border dividing Virginia and Tennessee, and the State Liners employed this quirk of Bristol into their team name. The State Liners played on the Virginia side of the boundary, lining up against the Knoxville Pioneers, Johnson City Soldiers and Cleveland Manufacturers.

1923 Bristol State Liners
—National Baseball Hall of Fame Library. Cooperstown, NY

Not to Be Confused With: Southern Illinois Miners

Between the Lines: Pasty O'Rourke managed the 1924 State Liners while his son Joe was an infielder on the team. Both father and son played in the Major Leagues.

LYNCHBURG HILLCATS

League: Carolina League
City: Lynchburg, VA
Years: 1995-Present

Lynchburg is known as the "City of Seven Hills" because of its location at the base of the Blue Ridge Mountains. Team management sorted through hundreds of team name submissions after the 1994 season and wanted their hilly setting incorporated into the new look. The Hillcats are now the High-A affiliate of the Atlanta Braves after stints partnering with the Pirates and Reds.

Not to Be Confused With: New York Hilltoppers

Between the Lines: Major League All-Stars Nate McLouth and Aramis Ramirez both played for the Hillcats.

RICHMOND FLYING SQUIRRELS

League: Eastern League
City: Richmond, VA
Years: 2010-Present

Flying squirrels are real animals. They're found in North America but not necessarily indigenous to Virginia. The Flying Squirrels team name was selected for the quirkiness factor. When the Flying Squirrels moniker was announced, Chief Executive Officer Chuck Domino said it gave his staff "unlimited avenues to creatively explore the identity of this team." CNBC's Darren Rovell took part in the name-the-team process, sorting through Internet submissions that eventually led to "Hush Puppies" becoming a finalist in the vote.

Not to Be Confused With: Elgin Kittens

Between the Lines: The Flying Squirrels hosted an entire 2011 playoff series against Harrisburg because the Senators ballpark flooded.

SALEM FRIENDS

League: Blue Ridge League
City: Salem, VA
Years: 1946

Their team name was hardly intimidating, but there was a reason behind the Salem Friends name selection. Beginning in the early 1900s, Salem's nickname was "Friendly Town." In their only year in the Class D Blue Ridge League,

Salem Municipal Field—former home of the Salem Friends —Courtesy of Brian Merzbach

the Friends befriended teams like the Mt. Airy Graniteers, Radford Rockets and Galax Leafs.

Not to Be Confused With: Reidsville Luckies, Danville Speakers

Between the Lines: Friends outfielder Edward Wayne had a magnificent 1946 season, hitting .403 to win the league batting title. Despite the historic year, Wayne never got a shot in the Major Leagues.

SUFFOLK GOOBERS

League: Virginia League
City: Suffolk, VA
Years: 1948-1951

The Suffolk Goobers cracked into the Class D Virginia League in 1949, trying to roast teams like the Petersburg Generals and Lawrenceville Robins. The Goobers team nickname is in reference to Virginia's peanut production. There are currently 3,000 peanut farms in Virginia, producing over 5 percent of peanuts in the United States.

Not to Be Confused With: Albany Nuts

Between the Lines: Red Treadway played for the New York Giants from 1944 to 1945, reporting to Hall of Fame Player/Manager Mel Ott. Treadway later navigated through 11 seasons in the minors unsuccessfully trying to get back to "The Show," including a year with the Goobers in 1951.

Washington

BELLINGHAM CHINOOKS

League: Western International League
City: Bellingham, WA
Years: 1938-1939

Baseball fans in Bellingham, Washington, hoped the wind was blowing out when their Chinooks came to bat at Battersby Field. Chinook winds are found in the northwestern United States and the western plains of Canada. The winds send warm gusts so strong they can boost cold winter temperatures. The Bellingham Chinooks didn't have a breezy time in 1939, finishing 40-102 in their second and final year in the Class B Western International League.

Not to Be Confused With: Myrtle Beach Hurricanes

Between the Lines: Players in the Western International League didn't wear batting helmets in the 1930s, but one Chinooks opponent could have used one. Vancouver Capilanos batter Ed Stewart swung and missed at a pitch in 1939 and knocked himself unconscious when he whacked his head with the bat on his backswing.

EVERETT AQUASOX

League: Northwest League
City: Everett, WA
Years: 1995-Present

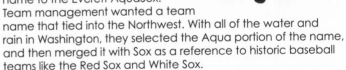

For a city with only three Minor League Baseball team nicknames in its history, Everett, Washington, has produced two pretty unique ones. Ninety years after the Everett Smokestackers played in the Northwestern League, the Everett Giants changed their name to the Everett AquaSox. Team management wanted a team name that tied into the Northwest. With all of the water and rain in Washington, they selected the Aqua portion of the name, and then merged it with Sox as a reference to historic baseball teams like the Red Sox and White Sox.

Not to Be Confused With: Welland Aquaducks, Dallas Submarines

Between the Lines: If there was a book about Athletic Trainer's names, longtime AquaSox trainer Spyder Webb would be on the cover.

HOQUIAM PERFECT GENTLEMEN

League: Southwest Washington League
City: Hoquiam, WA
Years: 1903-1904

There were no sportsmanship concerns when the Hoquiam Perfect Gentlemen played. Hoquiam has always taken pride in its hospitality and still uses the slogan "Washington's Friendliest City." The Perfect Gentlemen were close to perfect in 1904, winning 77 percent of their games against opponents like the Centralia Midgets and Olympia Senators.

Not to Be Confused With: Bonham Favorites

Between the Lines: The Perfect Gentlemen finished in a first place tie with the Aberdeen Pippins in 1903. When the Perfect Gentlemen refused to have a playoff to settle the tie, the Pippins were given the championship crown.

TRI-CITY DUST DEVILS

League: Northwest League
City: Pasco, WA
Years: 2001-Present

The Tri-City Dust Devils team name has gained popularity in the Pacific Northwest, but it wasn't the original choice, or even the second choice, when the team set up shop in 2001. The Tri-Cities in Washington are set nearby Rattlesnake Mountain, and the local name the team contest brought overwhelming support for the name "Rattlers." The problem was, the Wisconsin Timber Rattlers of the Single-A Midwest League cited copyright infringement, nixing the Rattlers name. After passing on the nickname Badgers, the name Dust Devils was selected. A Dust Devil is a miniature twister forming after severe wind.

Not to Be Confused With: Lake Elsinore Storm, Nazareth Cement Dusters

Between the Lines: Five years before starting Game One of the 2007 World Series for the Rockies, Jeff Francis pitched for the Dust Devils.

WALLA WALLA WALLA WALLAS

League: Inland Empire League
City: Walla Walla, WA
Years: 1891, 1908

Try saying this team name ten times fast. As Minor League Baseball teams began creating official team nicknames around the turn of the 20th century, some teams were behind the curve and used the city's name in their team nickname. Such was the case for the Class D Inland Empire League's team in Walla Walla, Washington. The Inland Empire League disbanded in July 1908 due to extreme heat, leaving fans of the Pendleton Pets, Baker City Nuggets and La Grande Babes without a team to cheer for down the stretch.

Not to Be Confused With: Trenton Trentonians, Lowell Lowells

Between the Lines: Two years after he was a Walla Walla, Piggy Ward set a Major League record while playing for the Cincinnati Reds. Ward reached base 17 consecutive times via a hit, walk or hit by pitch.

George McVey played for the 1891 Walla Walla Walla Wallas
—Library of Congress photo

YAKIMA PIPPINS

League: Western International League
City: Yakima, WA
Years: 1937-1941

Washington produces more apples per year than any other state, and an apple is even an official state symbol, so why not name a baseball team in Washington state after a type of apple? The Yakima Pippins, named after one of the 2,500 types of apples in the United States, played in the Class B Western International League. The Pippins finished fifth in the standings in 1939, rotting behind the Wenatchee Chiefs and Vancouver Capilanos that year.

Not to Be Confused With: Jacksonville Tomato Pickers, Beeville Orange Growers

Between the Lines: The 1939 Pippins had a team nanny. Nanny Fernandez started his career in Yakima and went on to play four seasons in the Major Leagues.

West Virginia

RIVER CITY RUMBLERS

League: Appalachian League
City: Huntington, WV
Years: 1995

The River City Rumblers rolled into the Appalachian League in 1995, playing in Huntington, West Virginia. The Rumblers team name relates to Huntington's role in freight shipment. Huntington is the largest completely inland port in the United States and is a major stopping point for cargo on the Ohio River. Railroads also use Huntington as a key anchor in coal shipment, dispersing coal from southern West Virginia.

Not to Be Confused With: Galesburg Pavers

Between the Lines: The most heartfelt story from the Rumblers roster was Julio Manon, who made his Major League debut at age 30 for the Expos after toiling ten seasons in the minor leagues.

WEST VIRGINIA COAL SOX

League: Frontier League
City: Wayne, WV
Years: 1993

Pioneer Field—former home of the West Virginia Coal Sox
—Courtesy of Brian Merzbach

You may ask why we would cover the nickname Coal Sox with teams like the Dublin Green Sox and Reno Silver Sox to choose from. With 270 coal companies and almost 600 coal mines, the coal industry is a large part of life in West Virginia, and the West Virginia Coal Sox became a creative and appropriate name. After the Coal Sox and Tri-State Tomahawks disbanded, it left the likes of the Kentucky Rifles and Ohio Valley Redcoats fighting for the first Frontier League crown.

Not to Be Confused With: Scranton Coal Heavers

Between the Lines: Rob Jackson pitched a shutout in the Coal Sox inaugural game and was later named Frontier League Pitcher of the Week shortly before the team folded.

WEST VIRGINIA POWER

League: South Atlantic League
City: Charleston, WV
Years: 2005-Present

The West Virginia Power took the field for the first time in 2005, the same season Appalachian Power Park opened in Charleston. This new era in Charleston baseball nicknames was motivated by West Virginia's energy production. The capital of West Virginia has used some unique team names over the years, like the Charleston Statesmen, Charleston Senators, Charleston Charlies, Charleston Alley Cats and the Charleston Wheelers, who paid tribute to Charleston's production of side-wheeler boats.

Not to Be Confused With: Mesa Solar Sox

Between the Lines:
Legendary West Virginia fan Rod "Toast Man" Blackstone starts

chants of "you are toast" after a Power pitcher strikes out a visiting batter. Blackstone has a toaster in front of his seat, and throws loafs of crispy toast into the crowd after each strikeout.

WHEELING STOGIES

League: Interstate League
City: Wheeling, WV
Years: 1899-1901, 1903-1913, 1915-1916, 1925-1931, 1933-1934

A team being named after a tobacco product may stir up debate these days, but for decades the Wheeling Stogies professional baseball team

1933 Wheeling Stogies
—National Baseball Hall of Fame Library, Cooperstown, NY

represented West Virginia's fifth-largest city. Wheeling was home to Marsh Wheeling, the largest cigar manufacturer in the United States. Wheeling is now the headquarters for Swisher International, which brands itself as having "America's Favorite Cigars." Stogie is short for Conestoga, believed to be the cigar of choice for travelers on Conestoga Wagons in the 1800s.

Not to Be Confused With: Lima Cigarmakers, Wilson Tobacconists

Between the Lines: Cy Young made his professional debut for Canton against Wheeling in 1890.

APPLETON PAPERMAKERS

League: Wisconsin-Illinois League
City: Appleton, WI
Years: 1909-1914, 1940-1942, 1946-1953

1913 Appleton Papermakers
—National Baseball Hall of Fame Library.
Cooperstown, NY

The Appleton Papermakers put their team name in print because of Appleton's paper industry. The city's first paper mill was created in 1853 and the first hydro-electric central station in the country was built in Appleton to provide power to the local paper mills. On the field the Papermakers stacked up against the Racine Belles, Green Bay Bays and the rest of the Class D Wisconsin-Illinois League.

Not to Be Confused With: Grand Rapids Cabinet Makers

Between the Lines: Former Papermakers pitcher Bill Cristall started six Major League games in 1901 and finished five of them. He was also the first Major League pitcher born in the Ukraine.

BELOIT SNAPPERS

League: Midwest League
City: Beloit, WI
Years: 1995-Present

Chris Parmelee —Courtesy of Beloit Snappers

The Beloit Snappers Single-A team is one of many turtle references throughout the city formerly called Turtle Village. Turtle Creek runs through the city limits, and Beloit borders a town named Turtle, Wisconsin. The various turtle mentions first hatched because of a turtle shell-shaped mound on the campus of Beloit College.

Not to Be Confused With: Memphis Turtles

Between the Lines: Four years before leading the National League with 50 home runs, Prince Fielder played for the Beloit Snappers.

CASPER GHOSTS

League: Pioneer League
City: Casper, WY
Years: 2008-2011

After the 2007 season the Casper Rockies dropped the name of their major league affiliate and inserted a ghoulish replacement. The Casper Ghosts team nickname was appropriately announced on Halloween, at a press conference that also unveiled Minor League Baseball's first glow-in-the-dark caps. Casper team executives had to clear copyright hurdles with Classic Media, the company that still owns the rights to the legendary cartoon "Casper the Friendly Ghost." Team CEO Kevin Haughian said at the time of the announcement his club is the only team in professional baseball looking forward to hearing "boos."

PBL trademarks and copyrights are used under license

Not to Be Confused With: San Bernardino Spirit

Between the Lines: The Ghosts filled Mike Lansing Field beyond capacity in late July 2010 when the greatest Colorado Rockies player ever, Todd Helton, arrived in Casper for a two-game injury rehab assignment.

CALGARY STAMPEDERS

League: Western International League
City: Calgary, Alberta, Canada
Years: 1953-1954

The Calgary Stampeders were named after the Calgary Stampede and Exhibition, an annual event with a rodeo bringing millions to the Calgary area each summer. The Stampeders were just one in a herd of unique nicknames this city has used for its professional baseball teams. Calgary's baseball history dates back to 1907, when the Calgary Bronchos chewed through the Class D Western Canada League. In 1985, in their first year in the Triple-A Pacific Coast League, the Calgary Cannons were born, and the current occupant of Foothills Stadium is the Calgary Vipers of the Golden League.

Not to Be Confused With: Buffalo Bisons

Between the Lines: Stampeders fans exhibited extra enthusiasm when Charlie Mead walked to the plate. He was the only player on the team from Alberta, Canada. Mead went on to play three seasons in the National League for the New York Giants.

Canada

EDMONTON CRACKER-CATS

League: Golden League
City: Edmonton, Alberta, Canada
Years: 2005-Present

The Edmonton Cracker-Cats are not named after anything you'd find at a pet store or grocery store. The Cracker-Cats bring up Edmonton's history as the "Oil Capital of Canada." A cat cracker is a chemical reactor used to convert oil. The population of Edmonton nearly doubled in the 1950s after numerous oil discoveries.

Not to Be Confused With: Thomasville Tomcats

Between the Lines: The provincial rivalry between the Cracker-Cats and Calgary Vipers reached a boiling point on June 13, 2006. After a lengthy on-field melee, seven players and both managers were suspended a total of 79 games. Edmonton manager Terry Bevington resigned after the incident.

REGINA BONEPILERS

League: Western Canada League
City: Regina, Saskatchewan, Canada
Years: 1909

1909 Regina Bonepilers
—National Baseball Hall of Fame Library.
Cooperstown, NY

The Regina Bonepilers was as intimidating of a name as we could dig up. Cree and Metis tribes originally hunted buffalo in the Regina area, and would stack buffalo bones in piles, with the theory that animals would not flee an area if they saw bones of their own kind. Stacking their way through the Class D Western Canada League against the likes of the Winnipeg Maroons and Moose Jaw Robin Hoods, the Bonepilers first played in 1909, just four years after Saskatchewan became a province.

Not to Be Confused With: Shenandoah Pin Rollers

Between the Lines: Cap Anson's hit total has been debated over the years because of conflict over transferring his National Association statistics, but some reports show a former Bonepiler, George Blackburn, surrendered Anson's 3,000th hit in 1897.

SASKATOON SMOKIN' GUNS

League: Prairie League
City: Saskatoon, Saskatchewan, Canada
Years: 1996

Saskatchewan was the battle ground for the North-West Rebellion in 1885, one of the deadliest conflicts in Canada's history. This part of history has shaped people in Saskatoon and also shaped the city's team nicknames, with names like Saskatoon Riot and Saskatoon Smokin' Guns. The Riot went up against the Brainerd Bears and Marshall Mallards in the North Central League, while the Smokin' Guns came out firing two seasons later in the Prairie League.

Not to Be Confused With: High Desert Mavericks

Between the Lines: Curt Ford delivered four hits and two RBIs for the St. Louis Cardinals in the 1987 World Series. He played for the Smokin' Guns nine seasons later.

VANCOUVER HORSE DOCTORS

League: Northwestern League
City: Vancouver, British Columbia, Canada
Years: 1905, 1907

1907 Vancouver Horse Doctors
—National Baseball Hall of Fame Library.
Cooperstown, NY

The first professional baseball team nickname in Vancouver also had the city's most unique team name, but the Vancouver Horse Doctors were not the last of Vancouver's baseball nicknames. After winning the Northwestern League in 1911, including a squishing of the Victoria Bees by 63 games in the standings, an overly confident Vancouver Beavers team changed its team name to the Vancouver Champions for 1912. After a stint as the Vancouver Mounties, the Vancouver Canadians debuted in 1978, which is the nickname Vancouver's team has to this day.

Not to Be Confused With: Temple Surgeons

Between the Lines: Horse Doctors manager Honest John McCloskey was quite accomplished in the game. He founded the Texas League, brought professional baseball to Arizona, and managed for five seasons in the Major Leagues.

Index

Cover Photo Credits:

Clockwise from top:
Terry Tiffee—Las Vegas 51s
    —Courtesy of Steve Spatafore

Mobile Oyster Grabbers Turn
Back the Clock Day
    —Courtesy of Mobile BayBears

Brandon Snyder
    —Courtesy of Frederick Keys

Tony Thomas Jr.—Waikiki Beach
Boys
    —Courtesy of Eugene Tanner
        Hawaii Winter Baseball

Rosenblatt Stadium—Former
Home of the Omaha Golden
Spikes
    —Courtesy of Omaha Royals

Brandon Taylor
    —Courtesy of St. George
        RoadRunners

Back cover:
Boss Schmidt managed the 1920
Kalamazoo Celery Pickers
    —Library of Congress photo

Acknowledgments

The following people were very helpful in providing background stories and images for this book:
Donny Baarns, Andy Barch, Blayne Beal, Greg Bergman, Dan Besbris, Alexandra Briley, April Catarella, Jon Clemmons, Nate Cloutier, Anthony DesPlaines, Jeremiah Dew, Pat Dillon, Tim Drain, Stan Duitsman, Phil Elson, Mike Feigen, Garrett Flowers, Mark Freeman, Kyle Galdeira, Tom Gauthier, Jim Gemma, Jesse Goldberg-Strassler, Justin Gray, Jason Griffin, Jon Groth, Avery Holton, John Horne, Tim Hough, Steve Hurlbert, Toby Hyde, Pete Intza, Marcus Jacobs, Paul Kennedy, Erin Kolb, Jeff Levering, Dave Lezotte, Randy Long, Teryl MacDonald, Heather Martin, Christa McElyea, Kevin McNabb, Matt Meola, Nick Merrill, Brian Merzbach, Nicole Meyer, Ryan Mock, Donald Moore, Aaron Morse, Ron Myers, Frank Novak, Anthony Opperman, Mike Passanisi, Adam Pohl, John Potter, Matt Provence, Ari Rosenbaum, Dave Sachs, John Sadak, Matt Schill, Jeff Scholfield, Steve Schuster, Travis Sick, George Sisson, Michael Tetler, Brad Tillery, Jim Tocco, Heith Tracy, Chip Travers, Carol Trumbo, Craig West, Michael Whitty, Tim Wiles, Amanda Williams, Casie Williams, Erik Wilson, Dan Zangrilli and Andy Zides.

I used dozens of books from Arcadia Publishing's Images of Baseball series and also the league record books of every active minor league for research. *Professional Baseball Franchises* by Peter Filichia and *The Encyclopedia of Minor League Baseball* by Lloyd Johnson and Miles Wolff aided my search for older minor league team names.

I would also like to thank Rob Neyer, Joe Rhatigan and John Whalen for their editorial advice.

About the Author

Tim Hagerty is a radio broadcaster with the Triple-A Tucson Padres in Tucson, Arizona. He has also broadcasted games for the Idaho Falls Chukars, Mobile BayBears and Portland Beavers.

He grew up in Canton, Massachusetts, a short drive or train ride from Fenway Park in Boston.

Hagerty's sports broadcasting work has received both national and regional Edward. R. Murrow Awards. He has also been honored by the Society of Professional Journalists, Vermont Associated Press, Idaho State Broadcasters Association and Alabama Associated Press.

You can visit his website: **www.timhagerty.com**.

About Cider Mill Press Book Publishers

Good ideas ripen with time. From seed to harvest,
Cider Mill Press brings fine reading, information, and
entertainment together between the covers of its
creatively crafted books. Our Cider Mill bears fruit twice a
year, publishing a new crop of titles each spring and fall.

Visit us on the Web at
www.cidermillpress.com
or write to us at
12 Port Farm Road
Kennebunkport, Maine 04046